A Duck's Tale
of Many Years
&
Guide to Our
Nooners

Karen L. Mason

Duck and Decanter books are available for order through Ingram Press Catalogues

Karen L. Mason
Visit my website at www.duckanddecanter.com/
www.karenlmason.com

Printed in the United States of America
First Printing: August 2015
Published by Sojourn Publishing, LLC

ISBN: 978-1-62747-143-5
Ebook ISBN: 978-1-62747-144-2

Dedication/Acknowledgement:

To everyone who has shared time with me; no matter how brief. For I believe it is the sum total of ALL our relationships that help carve us into our full potential.

Special thanks to:

Mom and Dad and the seed they planted in love and light allowing me to join you and our family on this earthly experience.

Ali, Jason and Logan; what a privilege to have done the same for you.

About the Author:

Karen L. Mason; second child, first daughter of a family owned business which has contributed over forty years to it's community, and continues to do so by serving yummy sandwiches to guests who have become like family, through the contribution of an intentionally focused team.

A spiritual explorer since childhood, she accepts each challenge life presents her and finds the gift it held. It is through coming self aware that she maintains a joyful and holistic approach to leading, living and loving in this life experience.

She currently lives in Phoenix, Arizona and continues to contribute to The Duck; along side her siblings while assisting each team member to find their place of giving and receiving during their time at the Duck. As a team, they are co-creating community that resonates in cooperation, personal growth and joy.

About the Book:

Duck and Decanter; the original food and beverage experience. Established in 1972, Phoenix, Arizona.

Written by a member of the original family; you'll find the history through the eyes of the eldest daughter, recipes to the sandwiches that keep guests returning, and a vision of the future through heart-based leadership in co-creating community. You'll even find a brief bed-time story to share with young and old alike, summarizing the events that occurred to make all of this happen.

Table of Contents

Introduction

"Welcome to Duck and Decanter. What can I get started for you?" With an infectious and welcoming smile, the Order Taker prepares to make notes on a brown paper Nooner Bag.

"Albacore tuna!" A happy customer offers with positive anticipation.

"What kind of bread?"

"Marble rye, please."

"Absolutely. Mayonnaise? Mustard?"

"Yes."

"Lettuce and tomato and cheese?"

"Yes. The Duck Way. Can you add avocado?"

"Of course."

"… and Champagne mustard instead of regular?"

"Yes. Anything else we can add for you?"

"H-m-m-m … pepperocinis, black olives, … and sundried tomatoes instead of fresh, Yum! Yes that's it."

"Nice job, and your first name?"

"Andrew"

"Andrew, iced tea or soda?"

"Yes, your blueberry iced tea sounds great."

"Excellent!" Order Taker hands him a beverage cup. "The 'Communi-Tea' Table is right over there, we'll call your name at the register, and you'll pay for it then."

Andrew walks away with a smile across his face, a cup in his hands and heads to pour himself a blueberry-iced tea. Two women step up next at the counter.

"Good afternoon ladies, what would you like for lunch today?" the Order Taker says with great joy. She loves it when she is scheduled right here during lunch rush.

Between two pieces of bread, real life, true satisfaction. Not just an ordinary sandwich, but a Nooner, hand assembled by one of Duck and Decanter's Sandwich Crafters.

The energetic sum value of over 40 years of experience, uncovering the magic of a vision while raising families, building relationships, creating a community. This is not just a meal, this life, shared by so many.

Energy. That's what it comes down to.

Welcome to "The Duck".

Our History:
Four Decades of Experience

Our original location circa 1970's

<u>To the Reader:</u> The events that unfold in this book are purely from my perspective and memory, influenced through the personal events and perceptions during that time. They are not necessarily the views of my family members.
They can write their own book :)

HOW IT STARTED

Earl and Dort just married

In 1954, my dad, Earl Mettler Jr, was first introduced to my mom, Dorothy A. Nylund, at an ASU (ASC at the time) Fraternity/Sorority function, Dad was with Delta Sigma Phi, and Mom with Alpha Delta Pi. She agreed to one date. He knew by their second date, they would wed.

"It was much more than physical, it was energetic, and it was true chemistry." Earl remembers. "I just knew we were to be together for the rest of our lives. She was 'real' and honest. She was emotionally mature. She wasn't 'playing games' like other young women of her age."

Mom excelled in her studies and obtained a degree in Education within 3 years while also tending to her responsibilities as a sorority sister and part of ASC's

Pom Pom Line. You could say that she really had it together. However, the truth was, she struggled most of her life with who her authentic self was, and what she wanted, until she met Dad. Dad saw and appreciated her for who she really was, underneath all that she had become, unrecognizable to her own self. Under this nurturing connection and deep love, Mom began to remember who she was and loved sharing the discoveries with Dad.

This specially matched couple married, and within six years, Randy, I then Tod came into the fold. Mom ran the well respected, Little Round Up Day School for children on 34th St and Indian School. Dad was working life insurance. Income from the day school afforded family vacations and land up north to camp a few hours away from the desert heat in the summer, or play in the snow during winter.

We lived in a cul-de-sac, on 36th place and Campbell where each of us three kids had friends either next door, or just a few houses down the road. We often played collectively Night Time Hide & Go Seek, Cops and Robbers on our bikes, or Whiffle Ball; bases perfectly positioned in the cul-de sac. We had two French poodles and two cats. We had chores, family meetings, school functions, and sleep over's. We each had a specific task in hand making our yearly Christmas Cards. My childhood was happy.

I was about nine when I first discovered the notes and drawings in Mom's nightstand drawer. A stenographer's tablet held the vision of a cafe. Notes were written as if requests to the Universe. The sketches showed what the menu would look like, and the words, expressed what kind of food they would serve. Dad loved to cook. My mom loved Dad. It was fun to hear and watch them "light up" when they talked about their secret vision. I could feel it energetically. It made me want to dream, to ask; what do I desire?

Well, corporate America snagged Dad with an opportunity too good to pass up, a new position, in a new state, with significant salary increase. They were willing to pay to relocate his family to Northern California. Excited for change, we soon found ourselves preparing to move away from the only house, neighborhood, school and friends I ever knew. From that quiet cul-de-sac on E. Campbell, we ventured to a new state, a new life.

Randy was somewhat reluctant to move away from his newly developed life and friends as a freshman at Camelback High school, Tod was hoping the change would help him to find a better connection with new friends, and I was finishing up 6th grade. Oh yea … during this time, 10 years after mom had given away all the baby clothes and furniture, Mom announced, during one of our weekly family meetings, that she was pregnant, Surprise! I was DIZZY with excitement for all the changes.

At the end of the 1971 school year, mover's packed up our belongings and we loaded up our 68 Chevrolet Carryall. The 65' Mustang had already made the trip. Down the road we headed, Dad, Mom, nice and round in belly, Randy, I, Tod, two monkeys (another story) two cats, two dogs and a guinea pig. We drove to the promise land of Marin County, CA. Life was moving quite fast for all of us, with bright anticipation of what was just around each upcoming corner.

It wasn't long after Jolynn was born that Dad regretfully missed the first few milestones of her early life due to travel. Unaccustomed to being away from the family as much as he was, it soon became apparent for Mom and Dad to make another change. As a family, it was not worth the material gain or success we had achieved. It just didn't feel right for Dad to be gone most of the time, life was much more than that. We were ready to return to Arizona, we were ready to come home to Phoenix. Back to familiar grounds, familiar schools, familiar friends.

In between careers, Mom and Dad's quiet vision still beat in their hearts, and saw that this could be the opportunity to do something very different. Is it possible to own something that what would be satisfying for everyone in the family?

After we quickly resettled, Dad scouted the Arizona Republic daily, not sure of what he was looking for, he knew it was more of a "sensing" what would take his breath away, what would make his heart beat faster. He knew he would "feel it" when he saw it. He trusted that, which he could not explain.

With now four children to provide for, anxiety rose for Mom at the same rate that our saved funds were diminishing. At the 11th hour, it appeared in the want ads of the paper. Dad saw its location and knew he found what we were looking for. Berridge Nurseries was our neighbor; Town & Country Food Bazaar was down the street and Cine Capri a little further down from that.

As long back as I can remember, Dad loved to cook a good meal. As a subscriber to Life and Gourmet magazines, he would regularly fix a Sunday "feast", often taking all weekend to shop and prepare. It would take varied stops to local shops to find the unique and necessary ingredients for his next creation.

This ... Shop ... is that place, where all of the items he needed; the spices, specialty meats, cheeses, wine, coffee, even the wok, garlic presses, crepe pan, and mandolin slicer could be under one roof. Back in the early 70's, only a few small local markets in Phoenix, and a handful for weekend chefs, were remotely familiar with what 'gourmet" was, Dad was about to change all that.

Earl and Dort 1975

In 1972, Duck and Decanter was nestled in the lush foreground of Berridge Nurseries, surrounded by rolling grassy knolls and tall palm trees. George Matonovich was the previous owner, who had this little shop for a few years prior. George was the one who came up with the name, as he was an avid duck hunter, and one of the few fine wine purveyors in Phoenix. His little shop carried a small deli case with a few meats and cheeses; he also retailed a few varietals of coffee beans and upper end cutlery.

At the time we purchased The Duck, there was no menu, only a few regular customers, who would offer to bring in their own bread then purchase a slice or two of meat and cheese to make a simple sandwich. Seeing the potential of this connection, we put a menu together, offering four handcrafted sandwiches made from quality products by a man with a song in his heart, and his wife. They were happy.

Italian Dry Salami	89
Imported Ham	89
Roast Beef	99
Turkey Breast	99

It wasn't too long after that, they added

The Whole Thing	1.25
Albacore Tuna Salad	1.25

Over the next few years, we listened and responded to the suggestions, desires and requests from regular customers, including the staff at "Berridge Nurseries" and "Lou Registers". Our menu grew. We used the phrase "Nooners" for our sandwiches, which now included

The Hot One.......................................1.25	
Fruit Salad	
(Adam's Apple or Eve's Pear)........................1.25	

We also offered a "Quickie", which was a Nooner, but sooner. Honestly, Dad, with his unique brand of humor, enjoyed playing off sexual innuendos. There were times when mom had to put her foot down against it.

By 1974, we were averaging 600 sandwiches a day, nearly 1000 on those spectacularly beautiful Phoenix weekend afternoons. Picnic blankets would cover the landscape, as families would gather to share their "Nooners" together. The sight alone was enough to pull traffic off Camelback Road, just to see what was going on. Duck and Decanter's name spread quickly. Regulars now referred us affectionately as "The Duck".

Customers commented how entertaining it was, just to watch the process of ordering and creating sandwiches. The Order Taker (Mom at the beginning),writing down your Nooner request on a brown paper bag, along with your first name, then placed in a box, where the next available sandwich maker (Dad), would pull it, and clip it to a rope, much like clothes to a line, to view while preparing it. After assembly, we wrapped the sandwich up in paper, and then slipped into its bag, and onto the counter. From there it would be stuffed with a pickle wrapped in foil, and a candy stuffed in a folded napkin. Then bag creased shut and lined up, ready for the cashier to call out, much the same way we do today.

Customers, while waiting could also browse among the retail aisles, intrigued and entertained by the varied and unique items we offered; unfamiliar houseware gadgets, specialty foods from far away countries, wines shipped in wooden crates, and coffee arriving in burlap bags. Items that encouraged consumers to try something different and new to their senses.

Mom and Dad were having fun, and passionate with the vision they manifested. The Duck created a "buzz", establishing a strong reputation for good food, unique market, and friendly family service,

Did you know the inventor of the sandwich was actually, the Duke of Earl? In the 17th century, Sir John Montague was a gambling man. He gambled so much, that instead of stopping for meals, he orders his cook to come up with a meal that could be served between two slices of bread so that he could eat his dinner with one hand, as not to interrupt his game.

FAMILY GETTING INVOLVED

Mettler Family 1980; Earl, Ruby, Dort, Karen, Jolynn, Randy, Tod

Everyone got involved, Grandmas and Grandpa, us kids as we could, and even a couple of Mom and Dad's close friends. My mom's Parents; Charlie and Dagmar, provided the start-up funds, Dad's mom; Ruby wanted to contribute as well, as best she could, cleaning lettuce each evening, making batches of Ruby's Fudge, (still available today) and in the evening, in her apartment, she would fold and stuff napkins with a wrapped candy piece, in boxes of 200. This was how we kept track of how many sandwiches we sold each day.

Randy, even before the age he could legally drink, was curious about wine making. Dad tutored him on how grapes were grown, harvested, and fermented. He educated Randy on the differences between climates, countries, and its effects on the wine. Randy's interest led him to gather more information by reading trade publications, searching out books on enology, and following industry journals. He also asked questions of customers and wine distributors much older than he. Soon he explored on his own, the subtleness between varietals while learning trade descriptors.

While his friends were drinking Thunderbird, he was wondering why convenience markets didn't carry Chenin Blancs and Rieslings. He joined mom and dad on trips to small wineries, tasting and tours in Northern California. Soon he was doing these trips on his own, building relationships with small vintners who were not interested in large distribution outlets. Sharing his discoveries, we became one of the first to offer wine tastings, and wine by the glass. He was happy and passionate.

Decades before there was a barista on every corner, Tod became Phoenix's first. After Dad bought a magnificent copper and brass espresso/cappuccino maker from Italy, Tod was inspired to develop the coffee department, accumulating knowledge of coffees, much the same way as Randy with wine. In 1980, Tod self-published our own "Duck and Decanter's Guidebook to Coffee", a timeless primer for those who were ready to branch away from the current trend and popular instant coffee powder to an enhanced coffee brewing experience at home.

We were daily brewing teas in glass gallon jars in the sun, which told the afternoon's time as the light amber color at 10am turn to a rich dark caramel color by three. By late afternoon, the tea would be strained and chilled for the next day. Not only quenching the thirst of our diners, but also enticing them to "try this at home". Tod expanded our loose-leaf tea selection and brought in a collection of unique accessories, such as tea balls, Brown Betty teapots, strainers, infusers and storage containers. He was happy and passionate.

As a toddler, Jolynn, too young to claim a niche for herself, became confident and comfortable interacting with customers at a very young age. Corralled during lunch rush to take a nap in her playpen, when she awoke and business was quieter, she was free to roam the retail aisles. Mom arranged inventory as not to cause too much damage when she wanted build castles out of boxes and cans. She became our youngest paid employee by learning to 'restock shelves 'and ringing up customers aided by a milk crate to reach the cash register. She was happy, as most children are naturally.

Me? My first job, during my sophomore year at Camelback High school (1975), was making sandwiches on the weekends. It was during my junior year, filled with school, social time with friends, homework, household chores; I also worked occasionally after school as well, getting familiar with our retail inventory. During my senior year, I was granted early release from school due to "on the job experience in career development", and started creating my niche in service at the Duck and with our customers. I partnered up with Mom, and we further developed our gift services from being the only Phoenix distributor of Knott's Berry Farm gift packs, to creating our own gift baskets with a wide and varied selection of foods, beverages and gadgets.

The main shift in my direction came from an inspirational 3am visit to the Los Angeles produce district, with Mom and Dad on one of our yearly buying trips. It wasn't long before we purchased a 15ft produce case, offering our guests exotic seasonal produce (everyday produce by today's standard) such as; kumquats, kiwis, lychee nuts, fresh herbs, parsnips, champagne mangos, cape berries, broccoli rabe, to name a few. We were also among the first to provide berries and peaches in December from faraway places. We built a kitchen during our first expansion. With four employees under my jurisdiction, it was my task to utilize the produce by creating recipes for soups, salads, desserts, entrees, appetizers. I was happy and passionate.

Mom and Dad were deeply satisfied watching their kids contribute to the business with such eagerness; giving us the freedom and room to expand our own visions, as we discovered and explored our natural talents and gifts. This entrepreneurship, perhaps, had become even greater than what they had first imagined.

Joy expressed through inspiration and passion was what our customers energetically felt. Yes, we created the best sandwich The Valley of the Sun had to offer, but it was also the "feeling" one experienced when walking through the front doors of this family owned and operated business. This was just as satisfying as our Nooners.

EXPANSION AND GROWTH;
WE WERE ON TOP

Duck and Decanter

Duck News

Arboleda	**Camelview Plaza**	**Heritage Square**	**Tempe City Center**	**Financial Center**
1651 E. Camelback	8800 E. Camelback	622 E. Adams	1420 E. Southern	3443 N. Central
Phx, AZ 85016	Scotts, AZ 85251	Phx, AZ 85004	Tempe, AZ 85282	Phx, AZ 85012
274-5429	941-5866	253-9780	820-8578	234-3856

Summer Issue 1988

Front Page News

photo by Paragon Resource Design

Rediscover the Phoenix Duck

Old ducks never lose their shape, they just flourish with new feathers, or so is the case with the original Phoenix Duck and Decanter. In October 1985, a new Duck and Decanter opened 100 yards south of the original site. The original Duck was closed due to a pending development of an office building. It was at this time that the Phoenix Duck moved to its more spacious quarters and began its flight.

This store is a prime specialty store and there is something for everyone. Whether you want a private intimate setting or a sunny spot for a large group, this is where you will find it all.

The upper level offers the majority of indoor eating as it overlooks the activities of the deli and shoppers below. It is filled with windows, displays, houseware items and features a traditional espresso/cappuccino bar along with a wide variety of freshly roasted coffee beans and bulk teas.

The deli is located on the main floor where you will find a Nooner sandwich being created to exact specifications. Browse through at the thousand and one gourmet items including the wine and beer room with its many domestic and imported selections.

Outdoor scenery is a major attraction of the Duck and Decanter, with the Phoenix store being no exception. Eucalyptus trees stand tall amidst the patio, leaving a perfect space to eat, talk or enjoy a bottle of wine while listening to a wide variety of musical entertainment.

The Phoenix Duck and Decanter, truly a place to rediscover.

Phoenix Arboleda Open House

The Duck and Decanter is proud to announce an Open House Party on the beautiful grounds of the Arboleda, 1651 E. Camelback Rd. On Friday, June 3rd, from 5 - 8 pm, **"Rediscover the Phoenix Duck"** while we celebrate the album debut of singer/songwriter **Steve Garcia**.

In addition to inviting members of the press and all our customers, we are featuring several wine and food distributors. These distributors will be presenting their products for everyone to enjoy. Wine samplings, culinary treats, beer tastings and our new iced drinks are among the specialties to be tasted.

At the center of this event, Steve Garcia will perform and debut his new album **"Copper Sky"**. Guest musicians will join Steve on our upper patio for an enjoyable musical performance.

Bring a friend and take part in Duck and Decanter's biggest event of the summer!

More on Steve Garcia Pg. 2

17

Karen L. Mason

Feature.......

Singer Offers Weekend Performances at the Phoenix Duck

From creating unique themes to developing new trends in the Valley, the Phoenix Duck and Decanter remains a leading source for weekend entertainment by presenting singer/songwriter Steve Garcia on Saturday and Sunday afternoons, 1-4 pm.

The combination of Steve's unique sound and the Duck providing live music was incorporated four years ago. Since that time the response has been overwhelming and is now a major attraction for those who seek musical diversion.

Steve often performs at other establishments and festivities, but most of his hours are at the Phoenix Duck. "I like the effect of the outdoor scenery, it gives the feeling of a concert and not a bar", Steve explained. He went on to say, "The crowd is very intelligent, open-minded and relaxed, they enjoy listening to my original songs rather the typical Top 40."

Steve is a California native who moved to Arizona several years ago. His accomplishments include **1987 Soundboard Magazine's Solo Performer of the Year**, plenty of media and booking attention and a new album titled **"Copper Sky"**.

Currently Steve is working on national promotions and is debuting his new album at our Open House Party. You may purchase "COPPER SKY" at Zia and Tower Records and at our Phoenix Location.

photo by Chad Copher

Department News

photos and trails courtesy of Arizona Republic

Squaw Peak Nature Trail - Length: 1.4 miles, **Elevation:** 1,800 ft; low - 1,540 ft. This is a self guided nature loop that includes a series of wooden posts describing the plants and animals of the preserve. Information booklets are available at the Northeast District Office or at the ranger station in Squaw Peak Park. The trail begins at the end of Squaw Peak Drive at the Apache Ramada.

Dreamy Draw Nature Trail - Length: 2 miles, **elevation:** 1,600 ft; low - 1,440 ft. This leisurely trail begins near the parking lot and picnic area in Dreamy Draw Park and includes a series of signs that pose questions about desert plants and wildlife. A corresponding booklet with the answers is available at the Northeast District Office. The nature trail also has a 1 mile children's loop.

CATERING

Looking for an exciting southwestern adventure this summer? Let the Duck and Decanter help you discover some of the historic hiking trails in our Valley and at the same time, keep your appetite satisfied. Begin your adventure early in the morning (to avoid the heat) and indulge in one of our several styles of gourmet picnic baskets. Whether you are with one friend or many, we will prepare a breakfast, brunch, lunch or even a dinner picnic basket. These baskets are complete with your choice of entrees, sandwiches, salads, pastries, fruit, cheeses, juices, premium beers and wines. All picnic baskets are complete with tablecloth, utensils, and wine insulator (if needed). A $20 refundable deposit is required. Call our Catering Department at 941-8835 for further information. Above all, take time during the early summer hours to enjoy the trails.

For your own free color map of all city parks and accommodations, call Kathy at 274-5429.

18

Department News

COFFEE /TEA

Don't let these hot summer months hold you back from enjoying a delicious cup of coffee. Use this time to take advantage of our coffee bar menu. This summer we are featuring two refreshing coffee drinks.

ICED CAPPUCCINO: Espresso coffee prepared in our Italian Espresso machine served over iced with a splash of white milk. **$1.25**

ICED MOCHA: Our Dessert Blend (Cafe Amaretto, Viennese Cinnamon and Swiss Chocolate Almond) prepared espresso style served over ice with a splash of creamy chocolate milk. **$1.25**

Both are served with a wafer

MEAT AND CHEESE

The Duck and Decanter is now presenting a **Cheese of the Month Program.** Come visit our various cheese departments to discover a new cheese or pate. We offer literature and samplings of these new products to further stimulate your palate. To be included among the favorites are **Les Trois Petits Cochons** pates and **St. Arnoix** smoked cheese. During the summer we will feature **Marcel et Henri** and **Delice de France** pates, also cheeses that are unique to their regions.

WINE AND BEER

We are proud to feature **Simi Winery** in June, as our Winery of the Month schedule continues through the summer. Please join us Thursday, June 2nd in our Scottsdale wine cellar when we will sample the wines from this fine Mendocino winery.

In the months of July and August, **Santa Barbara Winery** will be featured. In addition to the tasting of the lighter, crisper wines for which Santa Barbara is known, there will also be a special Zinfandel tasting scheduled.

Through the years we have relied upon the talents of trained tasters to assist us in the selection of our wines at the Duck and Decanter. We are now bringing those selections out of the cellar and putting our taster's reputation on the line. Each newsletter, they will select wines that are either exceptional values or excellent examples of the region or varietal; starting with:

Iron Horse '84 Cabernet Sauvignon $15.50
Folie a Deux '86 Chardonnay $22.00
Pecota Muscato di Andrea $10.95
Husch '86 Chardonnay $12.00

HOUSEWARES

Once again our nortorkous....
"20% Off Anything You Can't Eat, Drink or Plug In Sale"

June is the month to take care of shopping for family, friends, upcoming holidays or your own home. A 20% discount is offered on items such as cookbooks, picnic blankets, gourmet gadgets, cutlery and much more. An additional 10% discount applies to those purchases totaling $100.00 or more.

SPECIALTY FOODS

Key West Florida, besides being famous as the southernmost speck of land in the continental United States, is an island of wonderful taste traditions. Best notable is Key Lime Pie, a delicious, but surprisingly simple to make dessert that is famous for it's distinctive sweet-tart taste. The Duck and Decanter is featuring a product that will enable Key Lime addicts to have their pie and eat it too.

NELLIE & JOE'S KEY WEST LIME JUICE $2.85

Just what makes Key West Lime Juice so special? Unlike their green Persian cousins, Key Limes are small and yellow, with a distinctive, subtle flavor that lingers on the palate like a fine old Bordeaux.

While a remarkable recipe for "original" Key Lime Pie appears in this article, Key West Lime juice has many more applications. It is a favorite marinade for Ceviche. Combined with butter and a little white wine, it produces a fragrant sauce for almost any fish. Coming from the island of pop singer Jimmy Buffet's "Margaritaville", it's no surprise that Nellie & Joe's juice is an ideal ingredient for dacquries and of course, margaritas!

NELLIE'S KEY LIME PIE

14 oz can sweetened condensed milk
1 package (8 oz.) cream cheese, softened
3/4 cup Key Lime juice
1/2 tsp. vanilla
1 - 9 inch graham cracker pie crust
Whipped cream topping
 Place milk, cream cheese and lime juice in food processor. Process on low speed until smooth. Add vanilla. Process until mixed. Pour mixture into graham cracker crust. Chill in refrigerator until set, about 3-4 hours. Top with whipped cream before serving. Makes one 9-inch pie.
Please call Jill at our Phoenix location for additional recipes.

Deli

NEW FROM THE DUCK !!!

Beef Stroganoff $4.95
Gently Sauteed Beef in a Sherried Mushroom Sauce; Served over Egg Noodles with Seasonal Fresh Vegetables

Smoked Turkey Sandwich $4.15
Naturally Smoked over Hickory Chips and Free of Preservatives. We offer this, thinly sliced, with the usual choices of breads and condiments.

Pastrami Sandwich $3.85
Finally, due to overwhelming demand!!
Hot Mustard   (Select 1)   Coleslaw
Spicy Mustard   (from each)   Horseradish
Champagne Mustard column) Sauerkraut Relish
 Served with Cheese

Soup & Entree Combination
Your choice of any Entree with Soup
Small Soup 75¢   Large Soup $1.50

Karen L. Mason

20

Duck and Decanter

Duck News

Arboleda	Heritage Square	Tempe City Center	Financial Center
1651 E. Camelback	622 E. Adams	1420 E. Southern	3443 N. Central
Phx., AZ 85016	Phx., AZ 85004	Tempe, AZ 85282	Phx., AZ 85012
274-5429	255-5759	820-8576	234-3656

Fall Issue 1988

Front Page News

AN OPEN LETTER TO OUR FRIENDS

The Duck and Decanter is approaching the anniversary of our 16th year in business. When we acquired the Duck in 1972, neither Dori nor I could have foreseen the growth over the past 16 years. In retrospect much of this growth was spawned from a true love of the business and the challenge of providing customer's something different in product and environment.

Over the past three years the Duck has grown and expanded. We moved to the new Phoenix store at the Camelback Arboleda (behind Lou Register Furniture Store) and added the Tempe City Center and Financial Center locations. With the expansion we have naturally experienced some "growing pains" resulting in the closing of the Scottsdale store at Camelview Plaza. I believe time will prove this move to be beneficial to our entire operation as it will allow us to direct our creative energies into the existing stores. Many internal improvements have again enabled us to devote our attention to the positive aspects of the business.

During the ensuing months we plan to introduce new and exciting innovations. If you have not visited a Duck and Decanter recently, give us a try, you are going to enjoy what you find. From the beginning we have been proud to be the first to introduce new products and ideas to the Valley. This tradition will continue and prove the Duck and Decanter is "a place to discover".

We want to know what you think about the Duck and Decanter. We have a surprise gift waiting if you will take a few minutes to give us your views in writing. Stop by one of our stores with your written suggestions and a gift is yours for the effort.

The Duck and Decanter is a family operated business and there are 9 members of the Mettler family associated with the operation. This family attitude has filtrated our employees and it is one of the reasons the Duck is different from many food operations. I will close with one of my favorite stories about the Duck. When we were in the original store, a customer asked an employee if the Duck and Decanter was a family run business. The reply was: "yes, all 23 of us". This attitude prevails today so stop by the Duck and meet the family, all 70 of us.

Sincerely,

Earl Mettler

"Duck News" is a seasonal complimentary publication from the staff of Duck and Decanter to their favorite customers. If you are interested in adding your name to our list or wish to make comments regarding this publication, please do so by addressing "Duck News" 1651 E. Camelback, Phx., Az. 85016. This publication is not responsible for changes in price and stock that may occur. Editor: Kathy Cano - 274-5429 Publisher: Karen Rudd - 263-4321

Karen L. Mason

Department News

WINE AND BEER

The Duck and Decanter is a leader in wine education and tastings. This season our Phoenix Arboleda location is offering several seminars and wine tastings:

Introduction to Wine - This seminar will be held on six consecutive Wednesday nights beginning October 5th and will be conducted by Randy Mettler. He will be presenting a worldwide overview of grape growing and wine making styles. Cost is $120.00 per person in advance. This seminar normally fills early so to guarantee a seat, make your reservations in advance.

> **St. Francis Winery**
> Thursday, October 6
> **Kendall Jackson**
> Thursday, November 3
> **Burgess Winery**
> Thursday, December 1

The above tastings are $10.00 per person and begin promptly at 7:00 p.m.

Watch for our traditional champagne tasting scheduled for mid-December. Please call our Phoenix Arboleda location for further information.

MEAT AND CHEESE

Cooler weather means new pate and cheese selections. The Duck features a wonderful variety of bries and other soft ripening cheeses. For something light and refreshing try **Strawberry Cream Cheese** ($5.25 lb) on a Carr's Wheatmeal, ($1.25) you will find it to be absolutely delicious! Heartier cheeses include **Huntsman**, ($8.75 lb.) consisting of alternate layers of Stilton and Cheshire and is excellent with a red wine. There is also **Cotswald**, ($9.50 lb.) a Double Gloucester with chives and scallions which would make a great addition to a green salad. We have individual pates by **Marcel & Henri**, particularly good is the **Duck Mousse with Truffles**, ($8.75 lb.) Curious about the taste of a certain cheese or pate....? Just request a sample.

SPECIALTY FOODS

A TASTE OF JAMAICA Next time you are looking for an exotic and appetizing meal to prepare on your outside grill, try a jar of **Jerk Spice** ($4.65) from Cinnabar foods. This version of **Jerk Spice** was inspired by Jamaican roadside stands that serve jerk meat (a type of jerky, flavored and preserved with allspice or Jamaican pepper.) Cinnabar's **Jerk Spice** is a hot and spicy grilling paste that is a blend of peppers and allspice. It is in concentrated form as one jar covers four large chickens. It is combined with vegetable oil or wine then spread over chicken, pork or other light meats. After marinating overnight, the meat should be grilled slowly over a low even fire. A **Jerk Spice** entree is best when served with basmati rice, a green salad, French bread and of course - Jamaican's famous **Red Stripe Beer**!

GIFT BASKETS

It is never too early to think about gift baskets for the 1988 Christmas season.

What better way to present corporate or personal gift giving than with a Duck and Decanter Gift Basket? Our baskets are stuffed full with delicious combinations of wine, cheeses, fruit, crackers, mustards, jams, chocolates and much more! Discover why we are the Valley leader in gift baskets by sending one to a friend or relative for Halloween, Thanksgiving, or your favorite voter on election day.

Brochures for this years Christmas selection including discounts will be available by mid-October.

HOUSEWARES

Browse through our housewares department for a variety of continental baking ideas. You will find a diverse selection of traditional cast iron cookware, such as cornbread/cornstick pan, shortbread mold, plus:

- Swedish Plett Pan — $9.25
- Norwegian Krumkake Iron — $20-$24
- Italian Pizelle Iron — $27.00
- Danish Aebleskiver Pan — $7.25

DANISH DESSERT DUMPLING
(for use with Aebleskiver Pan)
2 cups buttermilk
2 cups flour
3 eggs
1 tsp. baking powder
1/2 tsp. salt
1 tsp. soda
2 tsp. sugar
Apple Sauce

Beat egg yolks. Add sugar, salt and milk; then flour, soda and baking powder which have been sifted together. Last, fold in stiffly beaten egg whites. Place small amount of fat in each cup of Aebleskiver pan and fill 2/3 full of dough. Place a small teaspoonful of apple sauce on top of dough, then barely cover apple sauce with a few drops of dough. Cook until bubbly, turn carefully with fork, and finish finish baking on other side. Serve with butter and maple syrup or jam. NOTE: AVOID spilling apple sauce in cups, as this will cause the aebleskiver to stick.

The Aebleskiver Pan is also a very useful egg poacher.

Recipes are available for all listed cookware items.

COFFEE/TEA

Cafe Le Semeuse - A coffee of impeccable credentials! 100% whole bean coffee blended and hand roasted in the Swiss mountains. Reduced air pressure enhances flavor development by utilizing less damaging heat. The roasted beans are then cooled in pure Swiss air and to insure freshness, **Cafe Le Semeuse** (reg. $6.25 & decaf. $7.25 for an 8oz. can) is jet-expressed in small quantities to the United States. This brand is truly delicious when brewed in any coffee maker or as an espresso. Available in regular or decaffeinated.

22

Fall Festivities '88

THE DUCK JOINS IN SPIRIT OF CARNIVAL PHOENIX '88

The Duck and Decanter is proud to kick off the fall season by being one of the sponsors for **CARNIVAL PHOENIX '88** (formerly known as Caribbean Carnival), September 23, 24 and 25.

The Duck and Decanter will be featured in "The Oasis", a large festooned tent with table and chair settings overlooking the CARNIVAL PHOENIX grounds. We will be freshly preparing and serving our famous Nooner sandwiches, along with a few extra surprises... Also included in the "The Oasis" is Alcapulco Bay Beach Club, who will be serving their delicious Mexican food. Musical entertainment for this tent will be presented by singers; **Steve Garcia**, and **Ranulfo Lemmus**, Latin guitarist.

Further ambiance is from the use of Environmental Innovations misting systems, plantings, and fine art sculptures.

Continuous world beat music on two stages will feature Latin, Caribbean, African, Mardi Gras music, and the distinctive steel drums and pulsating rhythms that are a Carnival trademark. A family picnic stage highlights children's shows. Duck employees will participate in the Siesta Bowl parade down Jefferson Street on Saturday morning at 10:00 a.m. The focus of the parade is humor, spoof and fun! The highlight of Saturday evening will be the Batucada Parade of Masks, a spectacular Pageant featuring 500 dancers and percussionists, a larger than life Phoenix Bird, with laser and pyrotechniques display for a grand finale.

Free parking is provided and prices are $3.00 in advance and $5.00 at the door.

CARNIVAL PHOENIX '88 is presented by the Akrun House in cooperation with Christown Lions Club and the City of Phoenix.

Duck and Decanter's Fall Entertainment Schedule

Don't let our sandwiches be the only reason to visit one of our locations, especially when you discover the Duck's fall entertainment line-up!

—— PHOENIX ARBOLEDA ——

Thursdays
Weekly rotation of three new artists:
Sophie Ozoneaux-
jazz/blues
Patrick Murillo -
reggae/Caribbean
Mark and Dawn Bowman -
classical/contemporary
4:30-7:00

Fridays
Vanessa Purdy -
folk/soft rock
4:30-7:00

Saturdays
Steve Garcia -
contemporary originals w/opening act
Devon Bridgewater -
violin and trumpet
11:00-4:00

Sundays
Steve Garcia
1:00-4:00

—— TEMPE CITY CENTER ——

Fridays
Hunt Becker -
classical guitar
5:00-8:00

Saturdays
Vanessa Purdy -
folk/soft rock
1:00-4:00

—— FINANCIAL CENTER ——

Fridays
Michael Collins
4:00-7:00

*occasionally performers will alternate stores

Karen L. Mason

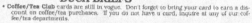
We were impressed how well our little shop had done by the 10th year. We successfully expanded the original location to include a larger wine room, with wine bar/cellar underground. Randy and I introduced "Dining at the Duck"; five course dinners prepared by

myself, and hosted by Randy who selected wines for each course. I also catered for private dinners and wrote "What's Cooking at the Duck" containing all the recipes. We built a real coffee bar w/barista, expanded our line of freshly roasted coffee beans and tea selections with additional brewing accessories. We fully integrated a specialty produce room that supported a full kitchen staff of six. We picked up our perishable imported cheeses weekly at Sky Harbor Airport.

National and local awards started rolling in and we received positive reviews from local food critics that recognized us as a leader of innovation in the public eye as well as within the industry. We were different from anything else out there, yet often compared to Zabar's of New York. We collected menus and brown bag samples from new local food places trying to replicate what we had done so well. "Imitation is the sincerest form of flattery." was our mantra. We started receiving inquiries to open up locations throughout the valley, a few of them, just too good to pass up.

Camelview Plaza at Scottsdale and Camelback, pleaded us to bring our concept to the East side. John Driggs, Phoenix mayor at the time, invited us to lease space in the historic downtown corner referred to as Heritage Square. We were asked be a part of the newest, hottest business corridor at the time, Central and Osborn. Tempe City Square at Southern & McClintock held such great promises of growth and exposure on land with plenty of green grass, and a manmade babbling brook and pond, filled with koi.

Between family and team members who felt like family, we had enough talent to spread our goodness out, and did so quite successfully. Family meetings were now about dreams, possibilities, and visions. Just how high could we fly this kite? All five stores were generating income. All five locations had great futures ahead of them. Mom and Dad, long ago having given up their role of primary order taking and sandwich making, spent their time visiting each location on a weekly basis; following up on progress, supporting managers, making suggestions on improving service, increasing flow, and advising on retail merchandising. We had reached a pinnacle. It was sweet.

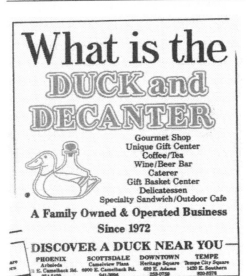

... AND THEN THERE WAS THE CRASH

It was in the early 1980's. I don't remember the specific details, as I was going through my own personal upheavals. Some suggested we developed too quickly. Perhaps, but it didn't help that three or our five landlords were filing for bankruptcy. Within a matter of a short few months, our vision of growth and development had vaporized.

Duality; the expansiveness of Creation was meeting its equally powerful contraction of Destruction. We headed towards Chapter 11. Randy stepped up and joined Dad to fight the dragons every day, trying to find leverage, somewhere, before having to completely let everything go. We ended up losing our personal property up north and my parents' home after filing personal bankruptcy.

Randy once admitted that during this time, there were mornings that nausea would sweep through his body as he prepared himself for the phone calls he had to face that day. Positive income flow had drastically changed its course on us. With no other choice, we shut down Camelview, Tempe, and Heritage Square. This narrowed us back down to two locations: the Camelback location, and Central/Earl.

The Camelback location was further challenged due to new land owners that wanted us to vacate. Our customers circulated petitions aggressively and successfully encouraged landowners to agree to our significance but forced to relocate south on the property, away from our curbside presence. Oh yea, Interstate 51 would be plowing through. In three years; between the move, and freeway construction, we became "out of sight". Many of our customers wondered what ever happen to us.

30 YEARS OF REGROUPING, REORGANZING

The years that followed these crucial challenges, gifted us the opportunity to painfully re-look how we did business, how our money was spent, how we manage our tasks and who was our customers. We looked at everything; costs of food, cost of labor, how to accomplish more in less time, what we could do without, how to reduce loss, and for the first time, we humbly admitted, we needed to look into how to market ourselves. As unique our concept was, by now the Valley was salt and peppered with similar niche markets.

We explored industry standards for support, but there were no standards for our unique kind of business. The closest match was "casual dining" and "specialty market", but to find standards that showed how to marriage these two concepts together was nowhere to be found. We created our own tools to increase efficiencies, decrease expenditures, tools to measure success and to capture and examine losses for future prevention. We study seasons and economic trends, in the hopes of sustainability for our customers as well as staff.

We avoided risks. We kept it safe, and played a sure hand each time. Slow yet steady. At family meetings, though we hoped for the best, we discussed and prepared for worse case scenarios. These meetings were not emotionally comfortable for anyone. We were asking each other questions that no one could answer. No one would admit hopelessness. We needed to become healthy.

We also listened to our customers; and responded through menu development. We added traditional deli favorites of our own version of egg salad, hot sandwiches, chicken salads, vegetarian options, and added bacon using Westphalian Ham. We expanded our breads, entrée salads, and side salads. We held a yearlong sandwich competition among staff and customers and came up with our "Signature Sandwiches". A simple menu that started with half a dozen offerings now was up to 40 items. Our expanded ingredient list, made dozen more combinations possible.

Randy, Tod, Jolynn, and I, now adults, were also personally experiencing many of life's blessings and challenges, as we created our own partnerships and families. Each of us left the business at different times in our lives to explore other avenues, and each of us returned with more to offer than before we left. For me, there were times when working at the Duck was a conscious decision, to be a part of its growth, by exploring my passion within The Duck; it was exciting. There were times when it was the Duck that supported me, offering schedule flexibility to raise kids as well as, perfect daily escape from husbands who struggled with their own definition of happiness. Scrambling to cope with all that had integrated into my life; I pursued other inspirational leads while raising my own babies into teenagers.

With each life experience I was presented with, through times of great personal humility, loss and despair … another story, I found myself looking at whom to blame for the maddening chaos that life can roll out. I admit placing the blame on The Duck was easy and convenient; asking questions like; what opportunities did I missed? Did the Duck deter me from my "real" life? "Why is this happening to me?" With no relief, I turned within, I returned myself to me. I reconnected with myself in new ways; exploring yoga, meditation, fasting, enjoying the benefits of nature, journaling, journaling A LOT, and reading, reading A LOT. I reconnected to Self and found satisfying answers to uncomfortable questions. My toughest self-work was exploring the limited beliefs I was holding on to, working them back to where they started from, and figuring how to release them, setting me free from their restraint. From here, I challenged myself to see everything through positive perception. I refer to this ongoing part of my life, as "Mastering My Truth"

Developing my tool bag for life, I was able to contribute to The Duck from a more expansive level, while continuing to see new ways to expand my awreness, new self-dimensions to uncover, to grow up, again, and to remember my Divinity, again. No matter what changes I experienced as an adult, no matter what storm blew into my life, the Duck, like a member of the family, always accepted me with no judgment. It was a time of maturing, not only as a business, but also personally.

THE PRESENT

YOUR ORIGINAL SANDWICH
AND BEVERAGE EXPERIENCE

Thirty years later we awoke from the humbling efforts of ... healing. Slowly we turned the ship around, now aiming for the sun, with the promise of the wind on our backs. We are remembering what it feels like to vision again, the magic of being passionate and new ways to be innovative.

We have had some tough decisions to make, and more to come. Between careful considerations, as not to repeat the past, bold steps into new ways of looking at business and finding our place within the community - my family, now including our own adult children, are moving forward. We are remembering the powerful feeling of inspiration that surfaced from deep within our parent's hearts at the beginning. We are taking risks again, and dreaming again, while tethered by rich knowledge only experience can teach.

For our staff, the Duck become an exploratory playground for each team member to create a self-satisfying experience and ownership by contributing their own unique talents. We encourage them, through opportunities that arise, to remove obstacles in their own personal growth. We encourage heart-based leadership, as we lead by example. We want them to enjoy the opportunities that this kind of empowerment provides. It requires all of our team members to be ready for their own personal examination.

We are exploring what our role is in the community, and what this integration looks like. We do this by reaching out to local non-profits, schools and businesses; asking how can we best serve. We are finding fresh ways to introduce ourselves to new neighbors, so they too will find a place to bring their loved ones. A business that survived and endured the challenges of being; divinely unique.

With the fertile grounds of passion expressed by Mom and Dad's ideas, plus each of us kids, and our own perspective gained through experience, we plant a variety of seeds by encouraging different points of view.

We continue to hold family meetings, but today it is more about how we each "feel" and what we can do to make our contribution to community enjoyable, sustainable, and profitable for everyone, especially our extended family; staff.

We hold staff meetings to decide as a group; a list of goals that will lead us in the agreed upon direction we head towards and the manner which to do this. We hold regular personal conversations with each of them, ensuring them the opportunity to create their level of participation towards our mutually established goals. Most importantly, we aim to ensure a level of satisfaction and joy that each member of the team can experience while working towards profit sharing for all. The Duck and Decanter remains much the same, yet different from ever before.

Our focus today is making conscious decisions. In purchasing we ask is it sustainable, is it consciously created, built, and made? Is there a local, organic option? When we interview for prospective new team members, we not only talk about beneficial industry experiences, but we ask questions such as what makes you happy, what are your gifts, what are your challenges, how do you stay healthy, are you ready for personal growth and how do you reach out to your community, as we promise anyone who works with us, a deeper understanding of self and others. We encourage that here. We are more conscious than ever before in the opinions of family members, staff, customers, and board members. We now understand that collectively, a higher level of consciousness in thought, word, and deed are the steps to true sustainability, in a world, we believe, heading in the same direction.

We recognize that co-creating community means authentically and emotionally connecting with each guest, vendor, and staff member. This has and always been the message behind the icon. With over four decades of experience, we have earned the recognition, for simply "being here". Enduring cycles of economy, climate, local and national governments, neighborhood development, market demands, global concerns … and raising families. These gold and silver threads make up our tapestry.

Our guests feel this, those who walk in for the first time, and those who have followed the traditions of "gathering at The Duck"; established by families, friends, and business associates. We have watched children run to the Treasure Chest (one free toy per visit), clamor up and down the stairs, under the watchful eyes of their parents, now grown and bringing in their own children, creating new memories. One can feel the warmth of nostalgia in a structure filled with decades of high vibration energy that resonates when you walk in the front doors whether it's your fiftieth visit or your first, coming "home" with each visit. A safe and familiar space, in a world as dynamic and seemingly chaotic as the one we live in now. Our loyal fans gather, for which we are so grateful, and is a pleasure to share and serve.

Our extended family, The Duck staff, is the glue that sticks it all together. As we lead each team member towards discovering their own personal gifts and passions, our intention is to offer a high level of satisfaction with their contribution, while sharing profits at the level in which they participate. They have the opportunity to unearth their perceived self-limitations, and let them go. They will uncover more of whom they really are. As they explore their authenticity, they are the ones who are creating new dreams for The Duck, they are the ones who understand that though compensation is gathered in wages, tips and profit sharing, of equal value is the experience they gain in sharing, and serving in a community they are co-creating.

Like family, they receive support and encouragement to find THEIR way in the world. Like family, each member encouraging, patient with each other's challenges, and appreciative of each other's gifts, celebrating in each other's victories. The path is created for committed team players to help manifest and share their vision and passion of the future. These are The Duck's new innovators, risk takers, and explorers, in a much different world than what it was four decades ago.

We are discovering the Duck's unlimited potential by releasing the netting around the webbing of its feet, of outdated beliefs based on previous struggles. Our guests are amused and delighted by the Duck's evolution, as we step into new territories, maintaining the values of what we all hold dear. It is a time of trusting, listening, risking a little, visioning a lot, and releasing our focus of past traumas. It is a time of remembering the path that created our success in the first place. A time to remember the dream, the passion, the joy of connecting with others in our community, sharing in celebration, maintaining THAT place that nourishes not only the body, but also the soul. This is what the Duck has always been. This is what the Duck continues to unfold into.

EACH FAMILY MEMBER'S
CURRENT ROLE AT THE DUCK

Dad, approaching mid 80's, has retired from his operational duties at the Duck, to focus on this stage of life, with limited mobility. Learning to partner with his body in a new way and the skills required, he is redefining how he finds satisfaction and joy. He maintains a sharp mind, respected perspective and opinion because of his valued experience in the Duck's history. He remains in active contribution to the Duck attending Corporate, Board and Shareholder meetings. His own gifts of intuitive abilities and sensitivities, following inspiration through the philosophy of his own truth, often sung through lyrics or limerick, which led him to purchasing the Duck in the first place. It is his humor, positive perspective, deep well of experience, objectivity, and clarity that supports, and humors the family and the Duck.

Mom, approaching late 70's, has learned how to become the caretaker, after all these years of being well taken care of by Dad. Now she is offered the opportunity to do the same for him, learning, and doing many things for the first time. Shedding her own perceived personal limitations, and embracing the powerful woman that she has always been. She assists The Duck, a couple of days a week, contributing in accounts payable/receivable, marketing, as well as our Storyteller and Counselor to staff and customers. She also asks the important questions to keep Dad in touch with the weekly pulse of the business.

Randy, with super broad shoulders, as mom and dad lessen their capacity, is learning to "think" less and trust more; holding for all of us, the bigger picture of financing, technology, marketing, and leading this family-owned business. Breaking through limited beliefs of the past, and one by one, letting them go. I have experienced and observed him reaching out and welcoming other's points of view. He is a fair man, whose heart is in a good place, asking important questions of all of us, like; "Because it worked 30 years ago, is it working for us today?", "How does it serve our community?" and "Are you having fun?". Excited about what the future holds for the Duck and the sweet changes occurring, passion has returned.

Tod is currently taking time away from the Duck, as each of us has from time to time; I most recently, returning from three years in Prescott. I can't answer for him, but I imagine much of it was similar to what I went through, examining who am I as a part of the Duck and more importantly, who am I separate from the deep long reaching cords of the Duck?

Acknowledging he was gay, during a generation where so much judgment and fear surrounded it was probably his greatest struggle. A struggle so perplexing that it was difficult to share it with his family. Yet he had the determination to express who he was, through the connection of his own tribe, community as well as kin, he continues to learn how to be authentic. Perhaps that is why he is further exploring today. Finding happiness, fulfillment and satisfaction, focused on a project he can call his own, or a new venue to re-discovering his gifts of diversity, varied interests, and unique perspectives that he was born with.

Transition seems to be the way of life for everyone in these times we live, Tod, is a humble reminder that change is inevitable, and with that, personal expansion. Each day I witness positive results of his contributions to the Duck over the years, and am grateful. I can vision the joyful prospect that he will find the perfect place for himself under the Duck umbrella, once again, and his family will celebrate in that.

Jolynn; even at a young age, definitely knew what felt right and what felt wrong. Being on the Debate Team and part of Mock Trials in high school and University of Arizona, she can be very clear about her beliefs, and it has served her very well. She has a strong analytical mind that balances a blooming nurturing side as she raises her own family. She is making a powerful position for future woman at Duck. Honoring the time you need to nurture your family without compromising your role as leader. She demonstrates that it is because of her female essence, she is a strong leader. She recognizes her blessings, deeply supported by her husband, Michael at home and at the Duck.

Me? The good Libra that I am, always seeking balance in supporting Randy at the Duck and Mom and Dad in their Golden Years while exploring my own visions and varied directions. I feel deep personal satisfaction as I move forward in "mastering my truth": through the lives I touch as leader, comrade, writer, sister, daughter, mom, aunt, friend, and lover. I am discovering the deepest magic that happens when one is truly connected to their authentic voice … and heart. I am passionate, that as I do this for myself, it reminds others to consider their own liberation. I believe we can create global peace in my lifetime. I believe we are that powerful. We all have the same choice; a perception based on love and trust, or fear and doubt. I choose love and trust.

As the fourth generation surfaces, now mid to late 20's…..my daughter, Ali and Randy's son, Pierce, are both contributing to the business, discovering how their gifts align and the most mutually satisfying way to share them. The Duck certainly offers them a very rich playing field for this kind of exploration. Ali currently dreams of a little vegan/vegetarian café/food space of her own, perhaps an extension of The Duck. Pierce is close partners with what inspires him, seeing where it takes him, in, around and outside The Duck.

I see a new kind of young adult emerging, those who are already plugged into conscious living. The younger generation, that surrounds all of us; are intuitive, sensitive, creative and exploring their own unlimited potential. Those who chose to find a place at the Duck, whether a family member or not, will flourish in new ways, partnered with the experience and wisdom the older generation holds. I can imagine a place for each one of my kids, nieces and nephews to participate in some capacity that fully engages and satisfies their own personal growth and life experience, whether they live here, or not. As our fourth generation enters, I suspect that they will find their way on and off the path of the Duck, just as their predecessors have.

Kids contributing elsewhere ... my two sons, Jason is a mixed media artist, working for Latitude 44 Catering in Hollywood, and Logan, attending Berkeley as an undergraduate in Physics. Randy's son Reed, living in New York works in the Learning and Development division at SoHo House. Though happy, successful, and accomplished in each of their lives, I gently hold sweet space that they may find a place at the Duck that will benefit from their gifts, even if remotely. There was one summer, when Jason was about 10, when he worked for a little cash. I asked how it was for him, at the end of the season. He said; "Mom there is one thing I do know, I never want to work someplace where there's a 'lunch rush'. An individual's life experience is fleeting, and determined by the soul that owns it.

Working with family is much the same as working with those who are not. It is about accepting beliefs of each member, while encouraging a feeling of positive expectancy in their own personal exploration. Accepting each one for their pursuit of authentic self. Honest discussion continues to be shared with all members of the family and the team. Well-expressed points of views are respected, and when differences arise, we have each become good listeners as we each aim to maintain satisfaction in a mutually benefiting way, and have fun doing it. Flowing forward into a world where the unseen actually takes precedence over the seen, requires much more trust, faith and personal development from each of us.

You ask; is it really this easy? Sure and there are times, when it's particularly hard. There have been times over the last four decades that each family member have asked; would it be easier to sell the Duck split the money and carry on with our lives. During our most challenging moments of sustaining this business, it has always been about connecting with the passion, letting go of limiting thoughts, and allowing circumstances to unfold. Sometimes that task is so hard, I ask, "Do I, or any of us, have the energy to welcome new risks, and change, again?", "Can I really help create new roadways to success without wearing myself down?"; "Can I honestly take each challenge as a grateful opportunity?"

Every morning, when I awake, the answer is always the same, "Yes." Because when it comes to the core essence of my job, my purpose, in and out of the Duck; it's really quite simple; To honor me, 100%. This means, holding joy and light, leading with compassion, follow inspiration, look for synchronicities, and be grateful. When I am operating from this space, honestly, it takes half the effort for twice the results.

There is also, this pull into what is right with the world, and a nudge into sharing it with whomever surround you; staff, customers, vendors, artisans, friends, and those who seem like family. The accumulation of experiences makes life rich; like cords of silver, copper, and gold in a tapestry, the Duck has validated and affirmed many of those threads for those who have entered our doors. Where longtime friends come to share a meal, grandparents meet their grandbabies for first time, widowers find comfort in a cup of tea; and teenagers succeed at their first job. Where other small businesses are born, lives of those who passed on are celebrated, friends playing weekly Scrabble, blind dates, girlfriends after school, and the young couple with their canine companion enjoying the Sunday paper on the patio.

When you find a place filled with kindred spirits that celebrate, support and encourage personal expansion and spiritual growth, a place that reminds us, life is good, we are safe, we are with loved ones, you have tendency to revisit and share such a place, often. This is the stuff older family businesses are made of. That's how you make a great sandwich.

The Food We Create;
A Guide to Our Signature Nooners

Sandwich Table of Contents

To all the Sandwich Makers who have contributed to the Duck ...

You have always been part of what propels us forward; leaving wide paths for others to follow.

We are grateful.

"Back in 2005, we were exploring ways to utilize Black Forest Ham in order to keep this unknown salt cured ham rotated and fresh. Customers were also asking for bacon. We discovered that when sliced thin and microwaved, this ham made an excellent, lean bacon."

BACON, TOMATO, AND CHEESE (BTC)

- ➢ Choice of Bread
- ➢ Mayo and mustard as desired
- ➢ 4 slices tomato
- ➢ Portion of Black Forest ham, microwave till crisp
- ➢ Cheese and lettuce as desired

Note: sliced turkey and avocado are commonly added to this pile of goodness.

"*In 2003, we finally satisfied customer requests for a duck sandwich, after our namesake. With the creative help of our beloved staff member; Marty; we created 'The Duckling'*"

THE DUCKLING

- ➢ Two slices walnut cranberry bread
- ➢ Evenly spread cream cheese on each slice
- ➢ Evenly spread Cranberry Relish on each slice
- ➢ ½ portion smoked turkey
- ➢ One portion sliced smoked duck breast
- ➢ Layer of spring mix & radish sprouts

"In 1987, in order to keep our inventory of brie and Proscuitto freshly rotated we combined the two together for this tasty outcome. It was first called the '5 ½', because in 1987, at $5.50, it was our most expensive sandwich.

THE BRIESCUITTO

- French bread, sliced open
- Spread Arizona Champagne Mustard on both sides of the bread
- One portion of Proscuitto, fluffed up
- Thinly sliced brie cut 1/8 - 1/4 inch thick to cover meat
- Layer of Sun Dried Tomatoes

TOMATOES, SUN DRIED

1 lb. Sun-Dried tomatoes
½ cup Olive Oil
1½ Tbsp. Minced Garlic

Heat olive oil in a large pan over medium heat. Add minced garlic, cook until golden brown. Add tomatoes, and stir to coat evenly. Add just enough water to cover. Reduce heat, cover and simmer for 15-20 minutes, or until most of the liquid is absorbed.

"In the early 80's our cheese department had discovered a delightful herb and garlic cheese spread imported from France and Genoa Salami for the first time. We created this delightful sandwich by combining these two flavors during a family picnic. By popular demand, we now make our own version of herb and garlic cheese spread.

THE GENOA

- French bread, sliced open
- Spread Herb & Garlic Cream Cheese Spread on each slice of the bread
- Genoa salami, folded
- Layer of spinach leaves
- Layer of Marinated Tomatoes

HERB & GARLIC CREAM CHEESE SPREAD

1 lb. cream cheese
1 Tbsp garlic powder
1 Tbsp Basil
1 Tbsp Parsley
½ tsp salt
Blend ingredients in food processor until smooth

TOMATOES, MARINATED

3 large ripe tomatoes
2 tsp olive oils
½ tsp balsamic vinegar
¼ tsp salt
¼ tsp black pepper
¼ tsp dried oregano
¼ tsp dried basil
¼ tsp sugar
Heavy dash of granulated garlic

In a medium bowl; combine oil, vinegar, and spices using a fork or wire whisk. Remove cores from tomatoes, then slice and place in bowl with marinate. Toss together lightly until evenly coated. This is top notch if allowed to marinate overnight in the refrigerator.

Our popular "Patio Tray"; a selection of cheeses and
meats, earning it's name as it is mostly enjoyed
on our patio, often with a bottle of wine, and
listening to live music, while the sun sets.

"In 1980, life-time staff member, Kevin, brought back a sample of Lebanon Bologna, from Pennsylvania, while visiting family. At the same time, Sugar Birdsall was also encouraging us to find a place on our menu for her new creation; Arizona Champagne Mustard. We married the two flavors together."

PENNSYLVANIA DUTCH TREAT (PDT)

- ➢ Dark rye bread
- ➢ Arizona Champagne Mustard
- ➢ 1 portion Lebanon bologna, folded
- ➢ Sauerkraut Relish, distribute evenly
- ➢ Swiss cheese

SAUERKRAUT RELISH

1½ pints sauerkraut, drained
1 cup Jamaica Pepper Relish, drained

In a medium bowl, thoroughly mix together both ingredients. Drain mixed ingredients into a colander for approximately one hour.

"In 1982, when we had a full staff kitchen experimenting with new creations, Dad brought in a recipe called 'Picnic in a Pocket', he had circled in a regional publication. With some adaptations to better utilize products we already had, we created this masterful collection of flavors."

POCKET SANDWICH (POC-?)

> ➤ Slice 1 inch off pita bread, separate carefully to form a "pocket"
> ➤ Evenly spread one heaping scoop Coleslaw
> ➤ Layer of pine nuts
> ➤ Insert and spread one portion of meat
> ➤ Evenly spread one scoop of grated cheese (we use a mixture of Swiss & longhorn cheddar)
> ➤ Evenly spread 2nd scoop of Coleslaw

My favorite vegetarian option is replacing the meat with avocado, adding onions, pepperocinis and black olives :)

COLESLAW

1 ½ lbs green cabbage, sliced
1/2 cup grated carrots
1-2 large leeks, sliced thinly
¼ head red cabbage, sliced
¾-1 cup coleslaw dressing (following)

Rinse cabbages, leeks, and carrot. Drain and allow to dry. Rinse chopped red cabbage under lukewarm water, drain thoroughly and add to large bowl. Combine all dry ingredients completely *before* adding dressing.

COLESLAW DRESSING

1cup Mayonnaise
1/3 cup rice vinegar
6 oz mango chutney
1/8 cup dried parsley
1/6th cup Russian hot mustard
1 tsp celery seed

Puree chutney in food processor until smooth. Gently process remaining ingredients.

"Poc-Ham"

"Being a vegetarian for most of my life, I was dissatisfied with the lack of creativity at any sandwich shop I checked out, in hopes of vegetarian options. I created this by using the veggies on our menu in the early 80's; introducing jicama from our specialty produce section."

WHERE'S THE BEEF (WTB)

- Choice of Bread
- Mayo and/or mustard as indicated
- Sliced celery
- Pine nuts
- 4 slices tomato
- 1 layer sliced cucumber
- 1 layer sliced jicama
- 1/3 avocado, sliced and distributed evenly
- Cheese
- Lettuce
- Sprouts

If a portion of meat is requested, place after avocado and before cheese.

Karen L. Mason

Circa 1972, this was our first Signature Sandwich. Adapted from a restaurant called "Ryan's Express" in Portland Oregon, we combined all the sandwiches on our menu at the time (which was three); ham, turkey and salami

THE WHOLE THING (TWT)

- ➢ Choice of Bread
- ➢ Mayo and/or mustard as desired
- ➢ 1 portion ham
- ➢ ½ portion turkey
- ➢ ½ portion Italian dry salami
- ➢ Cheese, tomato, and lettuce as desired

> *"In 2009, we had a yearlong contest to Create the Best Sandwich. This was open to staff members and guests. The following three winning recipes made permanent residence on our menu."*

VERMONT TREAT

- ➢ Spread Duck Cheddar Cheese Spread on each slice of Multi-grained bread
- ➢ Pine nuts
- ➢ Honey Glazed Ham
- ➢ One 1/4 apple, thinly sliced
- ➢ Layer of spinach

DUCK AND DECANTER CHEESE SPREAD

1 lb cheddar spread
1 oz port wine
1 Tbsp blue cheese
1/3 lb Cream Cheese
Heavy dash of Pickapeppa sauce

Set cheeses at room temperature, as it makes it easier to mix. Combine cheeses by hand. Add port wine and Pickapeppa sauce.

Note: Pickapeppa Sauce is a Jamaican style condiment and available for sale, or try Worcestershire Sauce as a substitute

<u>SMOKEY FOREST</u>

- ➢ In microwave, heat one portion Smokey Forest Cheese layered on top of one portion ham, to melt cheese.
- ➢ Spread mayo and/or butter on toasted ciabatta as indicated. (original winning recipe had both)
- ➢ Place heated ham and Smokey Forest Cheese on bread
- ➢ Black Pepper
- ➢ Layer of Tomato
- ➢ Layer of Spinach
- ➢ Vegetarian Option: replace ham with avocado

FIERY ITALIAN (FIERY)

- ➢ French bread
- ➢ Mayo and/or mustard
- ➢ 2 tablespoons Sicilian Pepper Relish
- ➢ ½ portion Smoked Turkey
- ➢ ½ portion Genoa Salami
- ➢ Provolone cheese
- ➢ 2 slices tomatoes
- ➢ Red onions
- ➢ Spinach

In 1983; it was originally called the "International Banger" because the ingredients came from around the world. English Banger Sausage, Swiss Gruyere, French Bread, Danish Ham, and American mustard. It was once awarded the "Best Gourmet Hot Dog" by New Times

<u>BANGER</u>

- ➤ Prepare French bread by slicing off top crust to create a "cap"
- ➤ Scoop out soft, inner bread to create a "cradle"
- ➤ Coat inside of cradle with mustard
- ➤ Place Banger Mix in bottom of bread cradle
- ➤ Heat Banger Sausage and place on top of Banger mix.
- ➤ Top with one portion Gruyere cheese
- ➤ Replace bread cap, and reheat in microwave

<u>BANGER MIX</u>

1 lb of ham, sliced and cubed
1 lb leeks
1 tbsp butter
1 tsp caraway seeds
Dash black pepper
Generous dash of mustard, powered
Generous dash of granulated garlic

Cut leeks into ¼ inch slices, soak to clean. Drain thoroughly in colander. In pot or deep pan, melt butter over medium heat. Add leeks and spices. Stir to combine thoroughly. Stir occasionally, until leeks are wilted. Add ham. Stir well. Cover and cook over medium heat, stirring occasionally, until ham is warmed through.

BANGER BROTH

1-12 oz bottle of pale ale beer
2 tsp beef broth concentrate
Enough water to cover sausage by 2 inches.
4 Banger Sausage (we use pork)

Mix well, the first 3 ingredients, add sausage, then bring to a boil. Simmer for 20 minutes. Serves 4.

> *In 1973, after our first year of operation, we created an 'au jus style' hot sandwich based on our family recipe for Swedish Style Beef Brisket. This appeased public demand to offer our first hot sandwich.*

THE HOT ONE (THO)

- ➢ One portion French bread, cut in half, then half again vertically
- ➢ Place bottom half in container, and cover with 2 tablespoons shredded Swiss
- ➢ Add one portion The Hot One Brisket
- ➢ Top with additional grated Swiss cheese
- ➢ Moisten the underside of the top portion of bread with juices, then place on top of meat and cheese and cut through meat and cheese.
- ➢ Include horseradish on the side

THE HOT ONE

5 lbs beef brisket, trimed
1 ½ tsp cinnamon
1 ½ tsp nutmeg
½ tsp ginger
2 ½ tsp salt
¼ tsp pepper
1 tsp granulated garlic
½ cup dark brown sugar
1 large white onion, sliced
1-cup dry red wine
1 bay leaf

Combine spices; rub into all sides of the trimmed meat. Place into a pressure cooker. Add wine, brown sugar, onion, and bay leaf. Cook under pressure for 40 minutes. Slice meat and replace into sauce.

The Wine Room at the Camelback location

What's a sandwich shop without their own version of this classic sandwich?

THE CLASSIC REUBEN

> ➢ Toasted light rye is recommended
> ➢ Spread 1000 island dressing on each slice of bread
> ➢ Fluff one portion of Pastrami or other meat choice to cover size and shape of bread choice, add one scoop Sauerkraut Relish and one portion of Swiss cheese (folded so that it does not cover an area larger than the meat) and heat to melt cheese.

SAUERKRAUT RELISH

1½ pints sauerkraut, drained
1 cup Jamaica Pepper Relish, drained

In a medium bowl, thoroughly mix together both ingredients. Drain mixed ingredients into a colander for approximately one hour.

Mom had a great burger recipe that we named D.A.M. Burger, after the creator Dorothy Ann Mettler. Dad could imagine customers ordering "The DAM Burger", and moved to a a family vote on whether to adding a grill in the kitchen. This was vetoed by the rest of the family. Thus, Tod and Mom "pulled" together this beautiful new addition to our "Hot Sandwich" collection in 2001.

THE D.A.M. SANDWICH (DAM)

> ➢ Slice bread in half-lengthwise. We recommend onion roll.
> ➢ Heated portion of D.A.M. Pulled Pork evenly distribute on bottom half of bread
> ➢ One scoop Coleslaw
> ➢ Place top half of bread on top of coleslaw

PORK BUTT RECIPE

8-10 lb boneless pork butt
Water to cover meat
1 Tbl Salt
1 Tbl Garlic powder
8 Tbl Pop's Dry Rub
2 cups Southwest Gourmet Jalapeno & Onion BBQ Sauce
Remaining juices in final roasting pan

In a deep roasting pan, cover meat with a brine of water, salt and garlic powder. Marinate in refrigerator for at least 12 hours. Remove meat and rub entire surface with Pop's Dry Rub. Place rubbed meat in shallow roasting pan, and fill bottom with "brine". Wrap entire pan securely with foil. Bake in a preheated over at 390 for 4-5 hours, or until it "falls apart". When cooled remove from roasting pan and "pull pork" into a bowl. Add approximately 2 cups of SW Gourmet Jalapeno & Onion BBQ Sauce to remaining juices from the final roasting pan. Mix well. Pour over pulled pork, toss Place marinated pork in the cooler - preferably overnight.

COLESLAW

1 ½ lbs green cabbage, sliced
1/2 cup grated carrots
1-2 large leeks, sliced thinly
¼ head red cabbage, sliced
¾-1 cup coleslaw dressing (following)

Rinse cabbages, leeks, and carrot. Drain and allow to dry. Rinse chopped red cabbage under lukewarm water, drain thoroughly and add to large bowl. Combine all dry ingredients completely *before* adding dressing.

COLESLAW DRESSING

1 cup Mayonnaise
1/3 cup rice vinegar
6 oz mango chutney
1/8 cup dried parsley
1/6th cup Russian hot mustard
1 tsp celery seed

Puree chutney in food processor until smooth. Gently process remaining ingredients.

Our Russian Hot Mustard often requested on sandwiches
and available in our Market to take home

In 1978, originally this was called "Beggar's Banquet" with a choice of either sprouts (for a protein packed adult sandwich) or jam (for the kid in each of us). It was, and still is, the most affordable sandwich on the menu.

PEANUT BUTER AND JAM (PB&J)

- Bread
- Generous portion of Peanut Butter on bottom slice
- Generous portion of strawberry jam or honey on the top slice (or try it with sprouts!)

PEANUT BUTTER

4 cups shelled roasted, unsalted peanut
8 tbsp. + peanut oil
Honey to taste
Pinch of Salt

In food processor, combine the peanuts, honey, and salt. Blend until peanuts become a smooth paste, while drizzling oil until desired consistency.

Note: Our Peanut Butter is now locally made, local owned

This sandwich is just as tasty whether its is freshly made or saran wrapped in your back for an energy lift on a long afternoon hike.

<u>TRAIL BLAZER (TRAIL)</u>

- ➢ Two slices cranberry walnut country bread
- ➢ Evenly spread 2 tablespoons of cream cheese on each slice
- ➢ 3 ounces Trail Mix evenly distributed
- ➢ 1 ½ ounces grated carrot evenly distributed
- ➢ 1/4 apple, thinly sliced.

Our Trail Mix is mixed and purchased through a locally owned business.
The Duck defines locally owned as within 100 miles from our front door.

This was part of one of our original menus in the early 70's, and still remains as the Valley's favorite. Available as either a sandwich or a salad. Mom and Dad's favorite additions to this sandwich is sliced pickle, red onions, and champagne mustard.

ALBACORE SALAD

- ➢ Start with a base of mixed greens
- ➢ Generous portion of Albacore Tuna Salad
- ➢ Tomato slices, and arranged around the albacore
- ➢ Shredded cheese blend arranged around the tomatoes
- ➢ 4 cucumber slices, cut in quarters, and 4 tablespoons sliced celery arranged on top of tomatoes and Swiss.
- ➢ Rice vinegar if desired

ALABACORE TUNA

2 cups canned solid white albacore tuna, drained
½ cup sliced water chestnuts, drained
¼ cup mayonnaise, heavy grade

After well drained, toss with mayonnaise, breaking up larger chunks of tuna. That's it!

Karen L. Mason

Another creation due to public demand

CHEF SALAD

- ➢ Start with mixed greens
- ➢ ½ portion each smoked turkey and honey glazed ham, cut into strips and placed in center
- ➢ 2 tomato slices, cut in quarters, and arranged around the meats
- ➢ 1/2 slice each of plain and jalapeno Havarti, cut in ½ inch strips and arranged around the tomatoes
- ➢ Black olives, sprinkled on top
- ➢ Feta cheese, crumbled on top
- ➢ Dressing of choice

Our version of a Taco Salad. Vegetarian alternative would be to replace chili with one of our vegetarian bean soups offered daily.

FIESTA SALAD

- ➢ Start with mixed greens
- ➢ Generous layer of spinach
- ➢ 1 soup ladle 3 Bean Beef Brisket Chili
- ➢ Spread layer of chopped tomatoes
- ➢ Layer of chopped onions
- ➢ ½ avocado sliced and arranged around chili
- ➢ Top with shredded cheese

When Dad (who always enjoyed creating sexual innuendos on our menu) first added The Fruit Salad in 1975, you had a fruit base choice of either "Adam's Apple" or "Eve's Pear".

<u>FRESH FRUIT SALAD (FS)</u>

- ➢ Start with a base of torn green leaf
- ➢ Generous scoops of Fruit Salad
- ➢ Four slices of apple, arranged at the corners
- ➢ 1/3 banana in ½" slices, arranged on top
- ➢ The equivalent of 3 medium sliced strawberries and one orange slice, arranged on top as garnish
- ➢ ½ Lazaronni Amaretto Cookie, crumbled on top
- ➢ 1 dark rye slice with Duck and Decanter Cheddar Spread, cut in ½, folded and wrapped
- ➢ Include a side of Poppy-seed Dressing

FRUIT SALAD

Watermelon, seedless
Cantaloupe
Honeydew Melon
Pineapple
Orange
Red seedless grapes
Strawberries (as garnish)

Rinse grapes and strawberries under running cold water. Remove rind any seeds from remaining fruit. Cut fruit into cubes approximately ½ inch in size. Combine all fruit in large bowl and mix thoroughly

DUCK AND DECANTER CHEESE SPREAD

1 lb cheddar spread
1 oz port wine
1 Tbsp blue cheese
1/3 lb Cream Cheese
Heavy dash of Pickapeppa sauce

Set cheeses at room temperature, as it makes it easier to mix. Combine cheeses by hand. Add port wine and Pickapeppa sauce.

Note: Pickapeppa Sauce is a Jamaican style condiment and available for sale, or try Worcestershire Sauce as a substitute

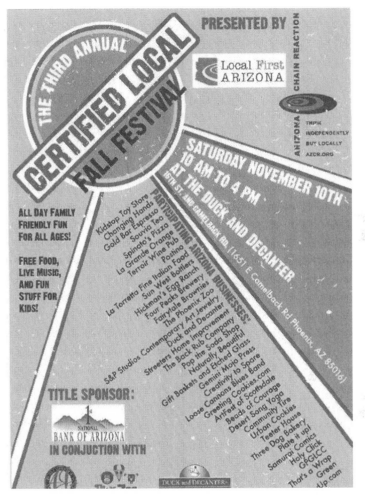

An annual event originating at our Camelback location.
Sponsored by Local First Arizona, continues today.

To "green" things up, we added our own version of this classic salad. Vegetarian option is to replace bacon with a generous portion of avocado. Yum!

SPINACH SALAD

- ➤ Salad container filled with spinach leaves
- ➤ Black Forest Ham microwaved till crispy for approximately 1 minute, then crumbled on top
- ➤ 5 Sun Dried Tomatoes, cut into bite-sized pieces
- ➤ Feta cheese, crumbled on top
- ➤ Include a side of Mustard-Poppy Seed Dressing

TOMATOES, SUN DRIED

1 lb. Sun-Dried tomatoes
½ cup Olive Oil
1½ Tbsp. Minced Garlic

Heat olive oil in a large pan over medium heat. Add minced garlic, cook until golden brown. Add tomatoes, and stir to coat evenly. Add just enough water to cover. Reduce heat, and simmer for 15-20 minutes, or until most of the liquid is absorbed.

MUSTARD POPPYSEED DRESSING

2 cups Poppy seed dressing
2/3 cup Arizona Champagne Mustard
Heaping Tablespoon of Seasoned Rice Vinegar

In a bowl, whisk together poppy seed dressing and champagne mustard until well combined. Whisk in vinegar slowly until desired consistency is obtained.

Introducing; Breakfast

First introduced in the early 80's. Lynn, a staff member at the time; quilted a huge 6ft x 2ft banner that stated "Breakfast". With a simple menu like 3 eggs with Havarti cheese melted, toast and green grapes and Day old Croissant French toast, we started breakfast. It didn't catch on at the time, perhaps because families were still finding time to have breakfast at home. Later reintroduced in 1990. Though sleepy in it's discovery, we are now known as the 2nd Best place to come for breakfast. Quality, conscious food in a quiet restorative environment with little wait. I suspect if we ever offer pancakes and waffles, that may change things.

It starts with three eggs and longhorn cheddar. You can either have it as a burrito or as a sandwich. If you want to get crazy; just look at the list of add ons. Serve with salsa on the side.

THREE EGG WITH CHEDDAR (3-E)

- ➤ Toast bread/warm tortilla
- ➤ Scramble 3 eggs
- ➤ Spread mayo and mustard if desired
- ➤ Place cooked eggs on bottom slice of bread
- ➤ Add longhorn cheddar cheese
- ➤ Serve with side of Salsa

HAM AND EGG SANDWICH WITH CHEDDAR (HEC)

- ➤ Toast bread/warm tortilla
- ➤ Scramble 3 eggs
- ➤ Heat ½ portion of Danish Ham
- ➤ Spread mayo and mustard if desired
- ➤ Place cooked eggs on bottom slice of bread
- ➤ Add warmed Ham
- ➤ Add longhorn cheddar cheese
- ➤ Place top slice of bread on top

<u>BACON (OR SAUSAGE)</u>
<u>& EGG SANDWICH W/CHEDDAR</u>
<u>(BEC OR SEC)</u>

- ➢ Toast bread/warm tortilla
- ➢ Scramble 3 eggs
- ➢ Spread Mayo and mustard on bread if desired
- ➢ Place cooked eggs on bottom slice of bread
- ➢ Add cooked bacon (or sausage sliced) on top of eggs
- ➢ Add longhorn cheese
- ➢ Add any extras desired

OTHER RECIPES WORTHY OF MENTIONING

CUCUMBER AND ONION SALAD

2 large cucumber, sliced down the center, then into ¼"
slices
1/2 red onion, slivered
1 Tbl Seasoned Rice Vinegar
2 Tbl Sugar
2 Tbl Salt
2 Tbl Black Pepper
½ cup Fine Herbs (equal portions of chives, tarragon,
chervil and parsley)

Toss to coat generously.

DELI TURKEY

1 # sliced and cubed Turkey breast
¼ of medium sized leak, slice, and rinsed
¾ cups sliced celery
½ cup walnuts (the original recipe used peanuts)
¾ tsp granulated garlic
½ tsp dried thyme
Heaping ½ cup of Blue Cheese Dressing

In a large bowl, combine all ingredients until well coated.
Add additional Blue Cheese dressing if necessary.

EGG SALAD

6 hardboiled eggs, chopped
1 pickle spear, minced
1 celery stick, minced
1 green onion, sliced (whites and greens)
½ Tbsp each; parsley and chives
1 tsp each; salt and pepper
2 heaping Tbl each; mayo and mustard

Mix well. Serves 2-3

GREEK SALAD

1 large tomato, cut into 1/16ths
½ cup thinly sliced red onions
1 cup black olives, sliced
1 cup quartered artichoke hearts, drained
¼ red bell pepper, chopped
¼ green bell pepper, chopped
6 Tbl olive oil
1 Tbsp balsamic vinegar
½ tsp oregano
½ cup feta, crumbled

Toss first 6 ingredients. Mix together oil, vinegar, and oregano. Pour over tossed ingredients. Add feta, gently toss one more time. Salt to taste.

FRUIT DIP (SERVED WITH OUR "CATERED" FRUIT TRAYS)

1 lb cream cheese, at room temperature
1 ½ tsp raspberry syrup
4 oz marshmallow cream
1/3 can evaporated milk

Whip well in food processor.

MARINATED ROASTED CHICKEN

6 roasted chicken breast
¼-cup olive oil
2 tsp balsamic vinegar
1 tsp black pepper
1 tsp dried oregano
1 tsp dried basil
1 tsp sugar
½ tsp granulated garlic

Over medium heat, mix oil, vinegar and spices. Marinate chicken breast 1-3 hours in the refrigerator.

RUBY'S FUDGE

7 cups sugar
1 lb butter
2-13oz cans evaporated milk
32 oz bittersweet chocolate chips
13 oz hippolite (marshmellow cream)
3 cups walnuts, roughly chopped
1 T vanilla

Line a shallow baking pan with foil or wax paper, or prepare 12-1/2 pound candy pans. Bring sugar, butter and milk to a full boil in large heavy duty sauce pan. Reduce to medium and continue to stir for approx 8 minutes, scrapping across the bottom of the pan to prevent browning, . Remove from heat. Add chocolate chips and marshmallow cream until well blended and smooth. Add walnuts and vanilla. Stir until well blended. Pour into one large pan or smaller candy pans. Refrigerate until firm

Earl's Mother; Ruby. Circa 1987

Karen L. Mason

Duck and Decanter
Team Members' Manual
(of the Near Future)
Zen, the Art of Crafting a
Nooner & Serving Joy

Note to the Reader:

The following is the authentic expression of ... me, Karen L. Mason. I struggled with where this part of the book was going to present itself. I knew the ethereal message I wanted to provide, but how to offer it in the most digestible way was challenging. I wanted it to flow with the facts of history and recipes, yet I also wanted to offer new insights, and an invitation to embrace the power we each uniquely possess.

After working through the fear of judgment from others, and my own personal self-doubt, I opened myself to freely receive this part of my book through Source connection. It is my intention to remind you of your own connection to Source, by providing inspiration through these words of light and joy.

Yes, the following is simply my perception, to which I ask; "What's yours?" We are our own creators whose building blocks start with thoughts, and the emotion that surrounds them, the mortar.

Having said this, I present to you, Duck and Decanter Employee Manual (of the near future).

My hope is that you enjoy the ride.

Congratulations!

If you are reading this, you have just begun your new experience here at Duck and Decanter. Some of you may feel a "stirring" with the words that follow. Consider that perhaps it comes from unearthing your current beliefs of limitations and an internal urging to set them free, shifting focus to your unlimited power. At some point during your interview, we promised you personal growth, to this invitation, you responded on some level, which resonates with you. This is why you are reading this now. Prepare yourself for transformation that working at The Duck will offer, with equal force as you put into it.

To succeed at the Duck, simply observe the different ways you best contribute and participate. Move towards the area that draws you in, the areas that will ultimately give you the greatest satisfaction. Communicate with the Scheduler or Talent Coordinator about your desires to help take the steps towards the places that best utilizes your gifts, and offers you fulfillment at the end of each day.

If you struggle with the exploration of finding your place at the Duck, noticing that, just "working" may serve you emotionally, positively in some way, then consider options with a team lead, store manager, or family member. We want you to succeed here. We want you to be engaged, to become confident with your contribution, satisfied at the end of each day that you made a difference, and did so with joy. We want this to be much more than "just a job", we want this to be a community you help to co-create, as you find your place in contributing to that tone. At the Duck, we choose to navigate towards the vibration of joy and positive anticipation.

:)

In the context of the following pages, I offer
Words and their Suggested Meanings

Density: Encountering a vibration lower than the current frequency one holds. This lower vibration can be a person or experience, anything we perceive through our five senses. Observing density while maintaining your personal frequency will offer insight into your own, expanded awareness. Finding something to be joyful about or grateful for will allow it to move through easily.

Duality: The cause and reaction to internal conflict between what Spirit knows as truth and EGO's judgment. Duality is currently what we, on Earth are experiencing, for a very long time. It is further supported through society and instant media. As we move towards our personal truth, duality dissipates.

E.G.O.: Earth Guide Only. Ego helps us move our body through this earthly experience and vibration. It helps us interpret our surroundings though our five senses. If used wisely, partnered with alignment of Soul's purpose, EGO can help manifest our dreams come true. When feeling conflict, it is because our EGO's interpretations are out of alignment with what our heart speaks.

Energy: The base element of EVERYTHING seen and unseen, vibrating at its own unique tone and expression.

Expansion: As we embrace experiences that challenge our current perceptions and choose to observe rather than participate, we can break through the limited thoughts that bind us. This raises our vibration. "Expanding" our awareness shifts from being "separate" towards being uniquely a "part of" the collective.

Light: Our highest vibration when fully connected to Source. As one works through their individual en"light"ening by observing then releasing density, we become unlimited. The opposite of Density.

Manifestation: A physical reality representing the vibration you are currently holding, whether you are conscious of it or not. When your vibration is of positive possibilities embracing your power as creator, with non-attachment to outcome, manifesting pleasant experiences becomes natural.

Resonate: Two vibration fields blending harmoniously together.

Shift: A change in perception that raises (or lowers) our vibration

Source: That which we come from, made of, and will return. That which is our ultimate expression. This comes with many names; Divinity, God, Universe, The Great Mystery are just a few.

Spirit: Our personal expression of Source that is housed, but not contained, in the "protective uniform" of our physical body.

Tone/Vibration: The rate of at which energy is experienced. Each of us resonate at a particular tone. It is suppressed, filtered, masked, or raised through the thoughts we think based on the belief systems we carry.

Unity: Being a part of a collective that resonates together; Home.

Zen and the Art
of Crafting a Nooner

Granddaughter; Ali Rudd making me, her mom, a sandwich.

Welcome to the Art of Crafting a Nooner, and serving the best sandwich possible, energetically transferable to our guests and community.

TRANSFERENCE OF ENERGY IN A PHYSICAL WORLD & HOW IT AFFECTS FOOD

Momma's Macaroni and Cheese, It's not the mac n' cheese that provides comfort, its Momma's nurturing energy as she was making it. How does it feel to create and share a homemade food gift, or receive one?

When food is prepared in a space of engaged and thoughtful intentions, offered in nurturing and kind service, then you have a high vibration dining experience. The body is receiving the maximum nurturing benefits, not only physically, but also emotionally and spiritually.

Have you ever noticed how easily responsive others are when they interact with someone who's joyful? Observe this with customers at The Duck, witness the energetic transfer of a hug, a soft touch, a warm handshake, a smile. Energy moving from one to another, THAT'S transference; nurturing both parties, because it is remembrance of who we are, a touchstone to Source.

At the Duck, the energetic exchange for the food, products, service, and experience we provide for our guests is currency. The same energetic exchange you receive for your contribution at The Duck. Can you see how beneficial it is then to experience consciously the process of raising your own vibration while working with us? It's not always easy, but as you become more and more aware, you soon will see the personal benefits outnumber the minor hiccoughs along the way. This is the personal growth promised, and asked if you were ready for, during your hiring process.

Before you begin your day with us, way before you clock in, take a quiet moment, whether at home, on the bus, or in your car; ask yourself, despite what appears in your life; am I feeling Joy? If you are; come on in, and congratulations, for you have made great strides, you have become well practiced at "shifting".

If not, take the time to scan your body and any messages it may be sending you. Any discomfort, imagined or real, physical or emotional, is a message expressing itself to you. Acknowledge and be responsive, yet practice releasing for now. Let go of whatever regret of the past or anxiousness of the future you may be holding, for Now is all there is.

Help provide service to our guests who gratefully offer monetary exchange for a satisfying meal, a memorable experience, an opportunity to realign and reconnect with their own personal flow. Trust that in your unique participation at the Duck today, you will be an important part in making this happen for them. Notice that in doing so, you are allowing the same for yourself.

When you clock in, acknowledge that this symbolizes the power within you to shift into positive realignment. That you choose to perceive the events that surround you as a joyful experience, an opportunity for expansion, as you release false perceptions of limitations at the back door.

Even the smallest shifts prepare the way for greater transformation. Observe that when you choose to feel vibrant, compassionate and joy, this affects the whole. As you park your car, lock up your bike, or before you get off the bus, scan your body, your emotions, one more time, encourage the open feeling that prepares you to fully participate in your scheduled time at the Duck.

Now and only now, please clock in and "in joy" your day with us. We are looking forward to your presence.

If you are struggling, and there will be those days, allow us to support your passage to feeling better. Consider your experience at the Duck today, a ripe opportunity, a safe place, to choose a different perspective to focus upon, a perspective that feels better. This is the personal expansion and growth opportunity we promised would occur. Magic will happen when you learn to "shift" your reality by recognizing the Creator that you are.

> *"When you change the way you look at things,*
> *the things you look at change"*
> *Max Planck*

As in life, and partnering contribution at the Duck, experiencing density is inevitable, as our society deeply supports duality. Be <u>grateful</u> for the lesson this conflict offers you. <u>Trust</u> that on some level, you have called this experience in, and will soon see the gift it represents. Remember the only thing we really have control over in this world we live in, is our perspective on any situation.

Four easy steps:

1. Let it go. Let go of your expectations of how things should be.
2. Change your perspective. Chose a point of view that creates an experience that's beneficial to you; Shift focus towards the unlimited possibilities and outcomes, instead of the existing perceived problem. This requires fun imagination.
3. Feel gratitude. Take a quick look around; focus on the many ways you are thankful.
4. Claim your power. Know you have just given yourself the power to CHOOSE what supports your expansiveness instead of the illusion of limitations.

Okay, sometimes these steps aren't so easy, let's back up just a bit.

YOUR TOOL BAG

FORTUNATELY! We each have tools to help us move forward, not only through the density of our earthly adventure but our role in its expansion.

Source. Our Life Force; that pure positive energy that cannot be contained, quantified, or captured with a label. It is unlimited; we just need to remember our ability to tap into it.

Heart (emotion). Our sixth sense, designed to remind us of our purpose, our gifts and the unlimited power we each possess. The more we tap into "Source"; the easier it is to navigate with heart.

Communicate With consideration, T.H.I.N.K. Is it; Truthful, Helpful, Insightful, Necessary, Kind

E.G.O. (Earth Guide Only) who's sole purpose is to help guide us within the physical limitations of earth, primarily through our five senses. As a tool, EGO assists in logistics, patterns, organization, and abstract thought such as systems, math, time, and structure. EGO and Heart are good bedfellows when Heart is used as primary guidance, through inspiration and vision while EGO handles pertinent logistics to take the action steps forward.

Meditation helps strengthen the voice of Heart and keeps EGO in check. Meditation is any form of action or non-action, focus or non-focus, which allows one to silence the mind's (EGO) chatter. Sitting in silence, while focusing on the breath, yoga, dance, knitting, hiking, biking, are just a few ways to experience this. Find what does this for you, practice silence for at least 10 minutes a day and it will transform you. Upon rising is a good time to practice experimenting with meditation, as EGO has not come to full reason yet, and you are closer to Heart's motivation, desire, and connection to Source. Meditation gives space for Spirit to offer counsel of highest regard for YOU

Free Will Our individual freedom to feel, based on how we choose to interpret our experiences. Blaming something or someone for how we feel is turning our backs on our abilities as Creators.

Each Other our compadres at work and the R.E.S.P.E.C.T. (Reliable, Enthusiastic, Supportive, Positive, Efficient, Caring, Team Player) that supports us as a team

MOVING THROUGH DENSITY; STRESS & FATIGUE

Each of us has experienced it; density feels heavy. It feels constrictive, burdensome, dark, tense, and tight. Usually brought on by the nudging of your Soul's expansive desire and an opposing limited belief, supported by EGO. Because society supports duality through its various media, it's guaranteed that duality will roll around, repeatedly, offering us plenty of practice to move through it. If we focus on the feeling of density, we are stuck. Eventually, it can shut us down.

As the evolutional energy around us speeds up, old perceptions of limitations challenge us. Being overwhelmed is inevitable; we physically feel stress entering our bodies from one moment to the next. Our breath becomes shallow, we lose our smile, and our inner dialogue supports the struggle we face. We feel disconnected from Source, our unlimited Life Force.

The magic is; we are all capable of "shifting" from this to finding freedom again. Going within and seeking peace, creates room for possibilities. Changing perspective opens space for solutions. Shifting focus towards positive change nurtures joy. When feeling light, free, playful, loving, we are at the doorway of manifesting the life we desire.

Regret or anger with the past, worry, or anxiousness of the future, forces you out of the present moment. This is what we ask you to leave at the back door before you come in for the day.

Nevertheless, there will be days where it will seem insurmountable. Perhaps you may be compromised in some way, physically, emotionally or spiritually, and events at home can compound discord even further. We ask that you shift yourself into the present moment with only your immediate task. This starts by simply being aware of your breath in and aware of your breath out.

Check in with your five senses. What do you smell, taste, hear, feel, and see? If in this moment of being here, now, capture one or two things you are grateful for and you will open space for peace to enter your day's experience. Be kind. Be respectful to your work friends and guests, knowing we all have "stuff" to deal with. We are all part of unlimited life force finding challenges living in a world of physical limitations. Developing and maintaining sensitivity to Source connection is a daily practice. Feeling the rumblings for restoration, detecting the first signs of discord, and being proactive to transmute it quickly to feeling whole again means we are remembering who we really are, unlimited.

Use your lunch break wisely by supporting the nurturing voice inside. Take time physically to be away from the business. Enjoy your satisfying lunch, writing/reading something uplifting, doing breath work, listening to supportive music, or quiet meditation. Maintain in the present moment with thoughts like:

"I have the energy to accomplish the tasks that need to be done today"

"I am well supported in the seen and unseen world"

"I feel Peace now"

"My only job is to hold Joy"

With this kind of practice every time you feel discord, distraction loses its momentum, while the voice of your higher Self becomes more pronounced and steady. It will give you more energy during the day. It will allow you to wake up refreshed, offer clarity in making decisions as solutions surface. Maintaining stability under stress, offers more smiles, and easy laughter. You will have a "way about you" that will make others attracted to you.

By moving through the density, you'll notice visions and possibilities become realities. What was once miracles move into everyday occurrences. Your purpose becomes clear, as does your gifts and the pathway to reach your highest potential. It is the moment-by-moment practice of guiding the flow of energy within you and around you that promises a life of joy, love, abundance, and light. It is easy to find communion with like-minded souls that further support this.

The other choice is mediocrity, regret, exhaustion, and confusion. Yet when you choose to be actively conscious with how you feel, and eager to take simple steps to restore and uplift, it doesn't take much to regain focus and inertia. It gets easier, as one continues to take care of the body while working with letting go, allowing, and trusting. MAGIC does happen, as your manifestations unfold.

Know that especially now in our world history-choosing happiness is more effective than EVER before. With just a small amount of practice, this shift becomes as natural as taking your next deep breath. We are bringing in experiences that give us practice to move energy. Retraining synapses in the brain, that once triggered doubt and fear, are now carving new pathways that shift to positive possibilities, achievements, loving relationships and joyful experiences.

Our existence is more than what is contained within the body. Being free is our natural heritage. As we learn to let go of familiar and old paradigms, they start crumbling underneath us. As we open our minds and hearts to new ways of thinking, we start to see the clear path to fully expressing the magical beings we are.

LETTING GO, ALLOWING, TRUSTING

What does one do when face-to-face with disappointment or despair? Conflict or emotional discord of any kind? Ask yourself this question; "What is it I need to let go in order to be present?"

Emotional releasing of an issue can be difficult, especially if holding it has become a daily project. Examining all angles to make sense of "it", and trying to figure it out is a directive of the EGO and does not serve a healthy purpose. Letting go of your hold gives space for healing or closure to occur. It is in the letting go, that in time, resolution, insights, and answers will surface.

If you struggle with letting go of a particular issue, "getting rid of stuff" on a physical level, becomes a symbolic step forward. Holding the intention of releasing emotional issues that no longer serve you, (even if you're not sure what they are) is a healthy practice.

<u>Try this at home:</u> Start with a small space, like a drawer, shelf, or cabinet to get the rhythm going. Grab three boxes and label "Garbage/Recycle", "To Donate" and "To Sell/Give". EGO likes the pile process, but allows the heart to "feel" which pile it should go into. Only make decisions that are easy and obvious, if unsure on a particular item, come back to it later. The aim is to create flow in the letting go process. Stay with distributing only those items you are sure about. After you have created some space, during the second sweep through, or third, you will feel clarity on those items you were once unsure about.

If it's garbage, toss it (or recycle). Give thanks for how it served you at one time.

If it's for donating, drop it off. Recognize the beauty of gifting to others.

If is for sale or gifting, and you have a lot in this section, consider a yard sale or a social gathering of favorite friends, work associates and family members to come over and "offer" what they think is appropriate for the item they desire. Remember the focus is not to get the best price, but to move it out; holding on for a fixed price will stop the flow of letting go.

As items are removed from your space, notice the openness, energetically feel the sensation of releasing, lightness, and freedom that comes from this exercise. Set the intention that with new space, there is now room for new opportunities, relationships, and experiences to flow in that will support you in positive ways. Allow some days to pass, and then take time to reflect the troubling issues that may have initiated this exercise; does it have the same hold? Or perhaps, you shifted your perception of it, or even have let it go?

By practicing letting go, you will develop sensitivity to conflicts as they arise, quicker at understanding the limiting belief behind it, and shifting into a better support belief, like pulling tender young weeds from your garden, to better receive your bounty.

"Just let go. Let go of how you thought your life should be, and embrace the life that is trying to work its way into your consciousness."

Caroline Myss

The next step; "Allowing" is our natural state of being, and an important process in the expansion of our self-awareness It is being "okay" with the feeling of nothing, in this busy "goal achieving society" we live in. It is in this space of "no action", which gives room for inspiration and creation. It has no measured space or duration; the process is simply to bear witness of doing nothing, and trusting that it is the natural process of creation.

"Allowing is the invitation to bring in the new,
the welcomed solution, the whisper of intuition,
or the gentle nudging of what action to take.
It is creating fertile ground for seeds
of inspiration to soon be planted."
Karen L. Mason, Master Your Truth

Then, "Trusting", which is done on a physical level, occurs every day. Trusting your heart will beat, your lungs will continue to expand and contract, every cell of your body is getting the oxygen and nutrients that it needs, and physical wounds will heal.

In this world, we control very little. With trust, peace becomes the foundation. Learning to trust takes courage and greatest leaps happen when our deepest fears in the dark are present and one either subscribes to it or trusts it as part of the process; trusts there is a message from Source or Spirit offering us a lesson. Trust is empowering your ability to choose how you feel. If trusting is uncomfortable - start over again, by asking; "What belief or thought am I holding on to that no longer serves me?

"Trust is like jumping off the edge of an
expansive precipice, safely strapped into a
parachute of your own Divine."
Karen L. Mason, Master Your Truth

Serving Joy

My nephew, Pierce, serving team member;
Lindsey a local brew after her shift.

CHOOSE YOUR PERCEPTION; CHOOSE JOY

There are really only two choices we ultimately make in every waking hour. We either choose to experience life through the eyes of love or through the eyes of fear. All emotions are rooted on one side or the other. Fear can reflect through anger, jealously, shame, envy, any emotion that causes discord to the tone of Spirit. Love can reflect as compassion, joy, forgiveness, playfulness, or the natural vibration of Spirit.

When faced with the many masks of fear, instead of examining why, ask, "How?" How quickly can you get to that space closer to Love, to feeling better? What thought, song, statement, image, friend, or word can get you there, the quickest way. How quickly can you let go of your focus on discord, and trust that true spirits 'tone' will seep into the space you create? In this space, check in with your perspective, ask yourself; are you seeing this experience that supports joy or one that supports limitation. What perspective, using your imagination, would bring peace?

It is from this position you are exhibiting power of the Creator within, and when you take steps for positive creation, soon enough synchronicities become dots along the right path to follow, resolutions occurs. We are awakening to the remembrance that we are free, that we are powerful. Despite the multiple ways society, and media supports amnesia, fear, and limitations, we are awakening.

It's quite simple; choose love. Choose to feel good. Choose to smile more often, and know it reflects in the circumstances that surround you, and those you encounter. It is from this platform we can practice the Creators we are.

> *"Our deepest fear is not that we are inadequate.*
> *Our deepest fear is that we are powerful beyond measure.*
> *It is our light, not our darkness that most frightens us."*
> Marianne Williamson

DESIRE → CREATION → MANIFESTATION

As you take on the challenge of personal growth by working with energy and moving through density, you are learning to develop your own personal power. You will witness that when you plug into "Source", a natural ebb and flow of creation and expansion develops, as you become more self-aware.

Before one can manifest, comes the position of Desire, most likely by experiencing what we "don't want" leads us to what we "do want". Though at first, uncomfortable, be grateful for this stage, and the gifts it will bring. Move quickly past the observation of what you are lacking and look swiftly and strong in making a clear statement of what you DO want. Ask yourself questions like, "What if I was in charge on my life?", "What if time and money were of no concern?" This will allow you to become more playful in the position of desire.

Once desire is clearly stated, focus not on outcome, but the feeling that comes from it, then the creation process has begun. This offers more practice with trust, knowing that progress is immeasurable by time or sequence. Simply become aware of opportunities that pop up, synchronistic events that occur, and complicated barriers that begin to untangle themselves. A pivotal phone call, or e-mail comes in, a comment made by a stranger or a decision made by a friend. Through these supporting events and circumstances, you will be led towards action. Trust the directional guidance from heart to lead you comfortably to that which you are creating.

Don't get stuck into the "how it's going to happen" or attached to the picture of the outcome, stay in the place of how the outcome feels. Neither let the structure of time or money stumble your process. Know when to let go, plant the seed of desire, and keep the ground fertile by quickly weeding any doubts that may surface. As your goal approaches, synergy works on your behalf; you will notice the feeling of positive anticipation, of flow and ease in perfect timing.

The "how's" are the domain of the Universe.
It always knows the shortest, quickest,
most harmonious way between you and your dreams.
Mike Dooley

Healthy body and lifestyle, defining your personal truth by focusing on life affirming outcomes, choosing positive perception of current circumstance, partnered with trusting, letting go and allowing, makes perfect alignment. This is the sweet place where MAGIC happens.

Synchronicities continue to validate your path and desire manifests very differently than imagined, unfolding in such a way, that Grace is the only word to define it. Sometimes the Creation process was so enjoyable; you haven't really noticed "it" has arrived, as it may have done so unlike any path you could have imagined.

After manifestation, the heart returns to a silent retreat of nothingness. It's not uncomfortable; it's just different from the active stages before it. In these moments, you are preparing the soil to plant again, further seeds of desire. It's only discomfort is when you allow Ego to try to name or categorize this place of "void". Take good care of Self. Be grateful. Listen to the inner voice that will lead you through it. In this void, observe the non-action in the nothingness. Know and trust this too is a part of the process. Soon seeds of inspiration and desire drop once again on the ground of nothingness.

The nudge will happen once again, follow it, and see what arises. Once again, you will return to the sweet abyss of creation, where no thinking is needed, just feeling the outcome you desire, following your heart, then inspiration to the first action that is being called. Follow that first small step, and you will see how it flows, quite naturally, gracefully, and joyfully. Be aware of this practice; it's fun :)

If what you desire, does not come into steps towards ease of manifestation; know that the core reason, is you may be holding a resistant thought that prevents you to move forward. There are times that choosing to stay "stuck" may be just what you need as it gives time for desire to ripen. Recognize as a conscious decision on your behalf, and take full responsibility. Be patient, knowing that works are happening on your behalf, mindful not to limit it within a time schedule. To take full responsibility for where ever you are at any moment in your life, gives you the power to create change in your life.

WHOM WE SERVE

The majority of our guests will arrive in good spirits, anticipating an enriching and nourishing experience. A small percentage will arrive unsettled, or out of sync; welcome them in, hold no judgments, despite what emotions they may bring in. Perhaps the possibility of transformation is what brought them in today. We can be pivotal in assisting them back to greater peace and contentment before they leave. Watch how a kind word, small gesture, or smile can make a difference.

We have created this welcoming place to enjoy good food in good company for nearly half a century. We did this by following our own heart's path. By working here; you have chosen the same path. Not only to serve up a great sandwich in a clean and healing atmosphere, but also to assist in that which refreshes and restores each of the guests before they leave. If perhaps something is not to their complete satisfaction, anyone, especially you, can step up and do our best to meet their needs. If you need assistance, just ask. Remember a small act of kindness can diffuse so much.

SERVING OUR COMMUNITY

THEY gather, they meet, they share, they celebrate, they dream, here, at The Duck. They are the youth soccer team after Saturdays' game, Happy Hour with co-workers on a late Friday afternoon, a surprise baby shower, networking events, study groups, lunch meetings, brainstorming committee, and common interest groups.

THEY are also the vendors we connect with each week, and their delivery drivers we have come to know so well. THEY are our local non-profit organizations that receive proceeds from many of our products and events. They are the local craftsmen, musicians, artisan, and cooks that we showcase. Our community is our local neighbors, businesses, places of worship, and schools. The Duck is a community icon because we do much more than serve GREAT sandwiches; we serve well-being, generously.

SERVING EACH OTHER

Know that each team member who have read these same pages, are exploring their own roles within the walls of The Duck and Decanter, while learning to release personal limitations. WE each become leaders when we use compassion, assistance, and kind communication in acknowledging each other's gifts. We each become leaders when we offer patience, support and encouragement when another may stumble through their own growth process. It happens to all of us.

We shift our understanding of energy as a team, when working together towards unity and flow. This guarantees we rise together to a level of success that will abundantly take care of everyone. We will also notice this accelerated evolution is happening everywhere, and discord only coming from those who struggle to let go of old thoughts and paradigms. The synergy of the team helps each of us, and our guests, to realign energetically in peace, cooperation, and joy, so as we create sandwiches, brew teas, pour a beer, make soup, mop the floor, or restock the shelves, our guests will feel peace, cooperation, and joy as well.

Your Team Leads will be in open communication with you through talent management discussions; coffee chats, and follow-ups to help you achieve your goals. We want you to be an important part of this team. If you need assistance in any of this, we are here for you, just ask.

YOUR SELF

When serving yourself with the heart felt intention of personal expansion and evolved awareness, then serving others and the community becomes effortless, and actually creates change and shift in a positive direction for everyone without even trying.

Use the Duck as a playground for personal exploration. Know that you have support, encouragement, and honest feedback. A place to uncover what your personal goals and desires are, a place where you can take those further steps toward your highest potential.

When it gets challenging, and it will; know that Divine resources and guidance are innately yours, in your moments of silence, just ask. Answers may come immediately, or may take time, simply be aware and trust they will surface. Look for synchronicities, pay attention to inspiration, or knowingness, that lead you in the right direction for the answers you seek. Once you have allowed yourself to be the awakened explorer that you volunteered to be, answers will arrive.

Anticipate unfolding events that support your desires by focusing on the positive feelings that the outcome will bring. Use your imagination to move into that place that creates the more pleasing thoughts, which give birth towards manifestation

Take a small action step forward representing your intention. Trust that your heart naturally seeks out the pathwork to remove limiting beliefs, and the Universe fully supports you.

In this practice, you will be creating new synapses in the brain. When doubt rises, a response to redirect becomes natural. Maintaining this connection to Source will have its ebbs and flows, the more sensitive one becomes to the energies around them, the more intuitive they become as they partner with this connection.

Remember this when you feel completely disconnected, ask what is needed to release. Give yourself time in nature, learn what you need to restore to that clear vessel that innately moves energy through easily. Occasionally, we all default to lower vibrations, where the comforts of old beliefs provide a reprieve from holding expansiveness and openness. This is a part of the evolution process of expansion and contraction, followed by expansion, then contraction, again and again. Recognize that your body is adapting to this acquirement of energy and that occasionally you may simply need to recess into your "humanness".

When you find yourself here; be gentle and kind with the words you use in self-talk. Be grateful for the opportunity to hold such a high vibration, and how it serves you to be connected to Source. The first step you take towards Source, starts with being good to yourself; physically, mentally, and emotionally; reminding you once again; **YOUR BEST ALLY....YOU!**

We are all moving towards full adaptation of our energetic potential.

As you move through conflict, holding on to none of it, the Universe is always supportive. Clarity and contentment will fill your presence. Transforming conflicts to positive perspective is easy, once you become accustom to recognizing the symptoms, and taking care of them right away. Experience conflicts, knowing that by using your authentic gifts, you can transmute them to positive outcomes.

Life is filled with challenges, more than some and less than others. Taking ownership of a perspective that you have chosen because of the lesson it holds, feels better than looking for whom or what to blame. The healing effects of humility are easy as well as the liberation in letting go. Observing your role by acknowledging your participation within life's hiccups will empower you to create change with courageous leaps of faith.

Then gratitude comes naturally, which creates space for joy. When "in" joy, we are all youthful beings, living on the playground of life, holding positive anticipation of your next adventure. Perhaps that's what being "forever young" is.

"Accept - then act. Whatever the present moment contains, accept it as if you have chosen it. Always work with it, not against it…this will miraculously transform your life"
Eckhart Tolle

Keep your body healthy. Choose your thoughts and perceptions wisely. Embrace the feelings that bring joy, transmute the ones that bring discomfort, and bear witness to the Creator that you are.

Understand circumstances arrive specifically for you so your gifts will surface as well as your path to co-creation. Friends that don't support your new direction will disappear and new ones arrive to celebrate in what you are uncovering in your Self.

Joy is an expression of love; the highest, purest, most powerful form of energy. It has healed across oceans in prayer; it has transformed others in a phone call, an e-mail, a thought, or vision. Many are seeking it these days of great transition and change, where energy is moving more rapid than ever before. Love feels of peace, and nurturing. Love heals, reenergizes, and creates space for new opportunities and fresh experiences. Joy is love, made manifest.

This is the gift that you give to yourself, to each one of your co-workers, and to EVERY guest that comes into the store whether you have direct contact with them or not. So powerful, it has the potential to affect the outcome of the day for our guests, even after they leave. Reaching your highest potential will do far more for global peace than any other action.

A JOURNAL ENTRY

Tuesday, December 16, 2014 AM

Wow! Just as I think I am truly grasping what life means and my role in it, cuz I have been so good at letting go old belief systems; BAM! Christmas.

I love Christmas, but it's a lot. Work, home, kids, siblings, Mom, Dad, extended family, friends, Christmas shopping, Christmas wrapping. What? No homemade gifts this year? Where's my "me" time?

I am sure my list is just like many others, and I am also sure that they will all agree Christmas … can be A LOT. Goodness, love, sharing, but also, for me, for whatever the reason; I associate Christmastime with what comes down to two old beliefs. 1. Not enough time. 2. Not enough money.

I was humbled; again, and grateful, cuz I've practice "becoming aware" all my life, and there echoes a familiar voice; "It doesn't have to be this way."

Reminders to Keep My Connection Flowing

Density. It will happen. Be grateful for it's reminder to choose your perception, in this this temporary moment. Remain unattached.

Be grateful for your body and all that it does. Listen and respond with only life giving action and kind words.

Every day; play, laugh, share, be silent.

Observe what inspiration feels like and practice following it.

With positive anticipation, expect success.

Make gratitude your daily practice and your bedtime prayer.

Treat all others kindly, with compassion and support. This will set you free.

Remember your only job; hold light, experience joy.

Be open to all possibilities that shift towards peace.

What are your reminders?

What It Comes Down To
A Summary

WHAT'S NEXT? ONE VISIONARIE'S PERSPECTIVE

Everyone in my family holds a vision for The Duck and their role in it. This is mine. I made a promise to myself at the turn of the century to step into my own authenticity. The words on the following pages are exactly that. From the Source connection within me. Namaste.

We (the family, and those that seem like family) have learned to step out of the encumbered ways of solving new problems with old ways of thinking, we have shaken loose old policies and procedures that no long serve us, and re-examined what we use to measure success.

As a family and business, we have courageously taken new risks, stepping away from a perceived reality of limitations, into a reality of abundant and prosperous possibilities through intentional living and business practices while co-creating community.

Our focus is building deeper connections by supporting local non-profits, local businesses, cottage industries, such as small farms, craftsmen, artisans, and locally created food products while continuing to provide high vibration food, service, and opportunity for our beloved quests and team we serve.

Social evolution has integrated in all areas of the store. Mindful of how we use our resources, we continually seek ways to reduce our carbon footprint, without compromising, what we have always done best; provide a memorable experience and an enjoyable meal. Standard practice like this is becoming a regional, and global occurrence, supporting each other, families supporting families, communities supporting communities.

As only one of the vision keepers in my family, the steps towards actualizing and manifesting this will prevail for itself when timing is right and we are ready to listen, feel, and intuit. Using our heart first towards transition, and our minds to create the path work, just as Dad did when he first discovered The Duck.

BE HAPPY!

Happiness is a choice. Consider this vision: Some place far, far away, beyond what our rational thought can hold, referred as Source, is a place we, as comrades, all came from, and eventually return to.

We were the courageous ones who were prepared and super excited to participate in this experiment called Earth; a place to use our own free will to share love, joy, and abundance on a beautiful planet specifically designed to support and nurture such an experiment. We volunteered to experience duality fully, by using our five senses as our guide through this limited dimension … our assignment: To assist in the world's shift towards unity.

We were excited to participate, because we had been preparing for this "experiment of the galaxies", transmuting duality and density. When we volunteered for this mission, if there was any apprehension, it was this; would we forget where we came from, that we are creators, that we are magnificent, that we are perfect just as we are? Will we remember our powerfulness through connection with Source?

We left kindred spirits of family and friends behind who fully supported our adventure, as they would benefit from our experience as well. For as we go through our years on Earth, they live vicariously through our emotions, free from the density, or separation. Our mission is not only to share this experience with our loved ones beyond this reality, but also mostly to help Mother Earth ascend. For Her time is near, Her time is now as we co-create Heaven on Earth.

In order to navigate our Unlimited Self through the density of this dimension, our Self is housed in a body, much like the protective gear an astronaut would wear, and perfectly designed to function on its own, along with five senses to help guide us through this experience fully. While in this body, be responsible, beyond everything else, take care of it. What you eat, drink, apply to the skin, breathe in, how you move it, how you rest it and how you "recharge" it.

Personally, as I honor my passion and follow my inspiration, life easily unfolds for me in the direction of my vision. I stumble only when I neglect taking care of my body. When I am mindful of what I consume, coupled with intentional living, I find I am enjoying a full participation of my physical evolution forward, with very little effort. The restoration my body requires comes easily, mindful moments such as walking, gardening, hiking, playing, biking, yoga comes naturally. Gratitude fills my heart each day and the desire to stay healthy is easy.

Perhaps, when enough of us are searching, exploring, remembering our glorious connection to Source, collectively, we move onward together. Perhaps we go Home, like a warrior after a very long crusade, joyously sharing our adventures with those who watched from a distance. Perhaps those who have struggled to learn or manage energetic expansion return, for further development, or perhaps come home to better assist us from the other side.

Much of life is such an exploration, with it, comes many questions, of which none of us knows the answers. The answers that I suggest give me peace; Give me opportunity to make a difference. Reminds me to evolve in love. To me, THAT'S what life is all about; mastering my truth is a process that I have always eagerly explored. Examining those ideals that deeply resonate with who I am, what felt like "truth" to me. Gathering these ideals, like seashells on a shore, mostly by taking on experiences deeply, validating through inspiration, intuition, receiving, and offering to and from those who come in to my life.

Just like the energy, that we are created from and surrounded by, mastering my truth will continue to be my journey as long as I share space on this Earth. Mastering my truth is not a destination; it is an adventure that I volunteered for a long time ago.

It is happening all around us. Energy is accelerating, and I can either try to tie myself down amongst the chaos, or let go and allow the movement to carry me to the most natural next progressive stage of shifting consciousness. This is a dance. I have stopped figuring out the steps, and have learned to just move to the groove, following the flow of inspiration.

Even in the mundane moments, there is a level of satisfaction and contentment that I cannot explain. When stress, doubt, or discord pops its head up, I am grateful for the message it is providing. I am grateful for the gift it left for me to unwrap. I start to witness beautiful changes and accomplishment with half the effort.

We are all transforming with the world in accelerated evolution towards more conscious living, even those who struggle, holding tightly onto powerlessness and limitations, are beginning to loosen up their grip, giving space for new possibilities. In the actions and thoughts, we each hold today, so does our family, where we work, and our community.

I feel it is my responsibility, my part of that mission I volunteered a long time ago, far, far away, to assist in Earth's ascension. I feel we ALL have an important role in Her ascension. As we move in our own energies to transform our own thoughts, eliminate our limiting beliefs, so it happens to those around us, it affects us globally.

As we clean our closets, someone is cleaning a shoreline. As we make peace with an adversary, two international enemies are shaking hands, and as we become empowered to recognizing our innate abilities to heal ourselves, so does Mother Earth. We are each uniquely and divinely powerful. It is easy to forget this when we give our power away to a person, dogma, ideology, what society thinks, or what the media is preaching,

My intention is not for you to join me in the beliefs presented here, but to encourage you, implore you, to pursue the mastery of your own truth. Make living a conscious decision.

We are the greatness of Source from which we have come from. Our light is immeasurable. You will never run out. You can never be severed from it. It is you. Always has been, always will be. Use it as your guidance to achieve your sweetest desires and greatest aspirations.

YOU ARE THE SAVIOR YOU HAVE BEEN LOOKING FOR.

NAMASTE

Trust the process. Trust the process. Trust the process.

And finally …

A Bedtime Story

The Princess
and The Duck

Photo Credit: AZJoe.com

"Do you have another story for me Aunty Sissy?" Natalie asked, not quite ready for sleep.

"Yes, I do. It's called The Princess and the Duck." Aunt Karen announced.

"Yes, yes tell that one again." Natalie settled into the nook under her Aunt's arm, with Elsie, her favorite soft toy snuggled under hers.

"Well, let's see how does it go again?......." Karen teased with a pause

"I know, I know...it goes like this..., 'Long, long ago, and not so very far away...'"

"That's right. Now I remember. Long, long ago, but not so far away there was a princess, who was still quietly tuck into her mommy's womb."

"What's a woom?" Natalie asked, knowing the answer, but wanting to hear it again.

"A warm and cozy space in the middle of mommies, where babies grow until they are ready to join us in this world. This princess ..."Karen continues, "could hear her mother's heartbeat, feel her mother breathing, and could hear all the happy voices on the other side, where her whole family was waiting for her arrival. The daddy, two brothers, a sister, two dogs, two cats, two monkeys, (which is another story), and a guinea pig named......"

"Jenny!" Natalie pleased that she knew

"That's right." Karen gave her niece a gentle squeeze.

"This special family was getting ready for changes on their own, for the daddy had a new job which promised a castle for mommy, new toys for his boys, and canopy beds and ponies for his girls.

It took many days, for the family to pack up their belongings, two dogs, two cats, two monkeys, and a guinea pig named Jenny into their long, long car, and a big, big truck. The daddy drove them, through the hot desert and over the mountains, to a land where everything was green and cool. The family was very excited about the new life that awaited them in the land of riches. They were excited about this new adventure.

When they arrived, their new castle was not quite ready, so they stayed at a local inn. It was very tricky, because this inn did not allow animals. So every day, while the daddy was working hard at his new job, the mommy, with her big, big womb, would load everybody body into the car and go on a picnic while the room was being cleaned."

"Even all their pets?"

"Yes even their pets. They had to be very sneaky sometimes."

Finally, the castle was ready, and just in time because before you knew it, the princess, having outgrown her own cozy room inside her mommy's womb, was ready to come out into her new world. She was ready to stretch and play. With so much going on outside, and hearing so many friendly and happy voices that said 'I love you', every day, she was excited to begin her new life.

Off to the hospital they went, and out the princess popped, so quickly and easily into the arms of her daddy. As she got settled in at the castle, her older sister was always peeking to see if she would wake up, if she had moved, or rolled over, if she was going to make a sound, if she would smile, and she did, she did all of those things. There were many things she was doing for her first time, it was so much fun watching the tiny girl grow, for they have never had a baby sister all their own.

As time went on her daddy continued to be very busy, working almost every day. The mommy was packing lunches and baking cookies, almost every day. Her brothers and sister were riding their bikes to school almost every day and excited to return home, especially her sister, to see what the princess did new. Did she open her eyes, did she smile, did she lift up her head, and did she laugh for the first time? And every day they would see something new.

Soon the Daddy noticed he was so busy working, trying to find ponies and canopy beds for his girls that he was missing all the new things his youngest princess was doing because he was gone most of the time. This made him sad, it made the mommy sad. It was time to stop leaving, and time to start staying home. The girls no longer wanted ponies and canopy beds. They just wanted him home.

He quit his job, and they sold their castle, and then said good-bye to all their new neighbors and friends. They packed up the long, long car and the big, big truck, once again, this time with two boys, AND two girls, two dogs, two cats, and a guinea pig named Jenny."

"What happened to the two monkeys?"

"The monkeys found a new home, as mommy said they had enough monkeys in the family. She was poking daddy when she said this."

"Why was she poking the daddy?

"Because he was the biggest monkey of them all." Aunty Karen gave her niece a little poking of her own, who giggled with glee, then settled back into her Aunt.

"Away they drove. Away from the green valley and the coolness of the mountains, down into the hot desert and finally they arrived pretty much where they left off, except this time, they had a new princess in the family."

"And no monkeys." Natalie reported.

"And no monkeys." Karen confirmed

"What did they do then?"

"The mommy and daddy said it was time for them to build their own dream. They had talked about it before, many years ago, and started talking about it again. It felt right, it felt good, and it was fun to think about it. It made them happy.

So the daddy started looking high, and low, looking for something he was sure would point them in the right direction. He didn't know what it would be, but knew that when he found it, it would feel right. It would make him smile.

But with no job, even the mommy was a little nervous because soon they would be out of the money they had saved. It was just about that time, when one very special day, the sun was shining so sweetly on a chilly November morning, the daddy was reading the newspaper, and saw this:

Small Gourmet Store for Sale by Owner
Must move. Sale quickly.
16th st and Camelback
602-274-5429

When he read this, he knew he had found what he had been searching for. He knew this because he felt this smile on his face so big that even his heart was smiling."

"What was it called, what was it called?"

"Sweetie you know the answer to that"

"Yes! Duck and Decanter! And the princess is my momma, right?"

"Right! The daddy, mommy, brothers, and sister were all able to 'play store' all day long, every day, and the little princess played wherever she wanted too. People came from miles around every day to spread their picnic blankets on the green grass, buy special sandwiches, snacks, and drinks that this family was there to prepare and serve. Everyone lived happily ever after because they chose to find happiness by trusting their dreams.

"Aunty Sissy, will I ever work at the Duck?"

"If you want to."

"I do!"

"We'll see" she said with a wink.

End

:)

Back Row: Tod, Randy, Jill, Earl, Michael
Front Row: Pierce, Karen, Ali, Dort, Jolynn, Natalie

In Gratitude

Dad, Mom, Randy, Tod, Jolynn and extended family; thank-you for your seeds of inspiration, roots of courage, and carrying so much of the load for those you love. You have each shined light on my self-created limitations, while offering acceptance, patience and compassion as I gathered the courage to set them free. Thank-you each for being such a pleasant surprise in this family and sharing your own beautiful gifts as you uncovered them.

My kids; Ali, Jason and Logan; thank-you for choosing me to be the vessel for your spirit to travel through. It has been an honor, and I am filled with pride and joy to watch each one of you discover your own way through this beautiful Earth assignment that you have signed up for.

The Duck; a place where we ALL gather, to simply BE. I am so grateful we have had you; for my family, friends and community to come to, refresh and grow during these intense times of change we live in.

Our guests and staff: thank-you for raising me in your inevitable style and grace, while accepting my authenticity. It is always such a pleasure to connect with each of you.

Prescott Friends; thank-you for your careful parenting, and allowing this child to enter your hearts then leave your city. Prescott will always remain a special place to me.

Past, present, and future lovers for allowing me to fully and deeply hold the dimensions of love expressed on a physical level. You have been some of my greatest guides towards who I am.

Special Thanks To Michael, Jeff and Joe. One who helped me to create three beautiful children, one who forced me to see myself clearly and the other who demonstrated it is good to rejoice in what I see.

Mother Earth; and the playground she has given us to explore and practice healing on so many levels.

Source; for this super rich experience we call LIFE. I have gone through enough of them to show that the binds I impose on myself, are blessed with experiences that set them free. I AM FREE to choose uncomfortable circumstances supported by limited beliefs and I AM FREE to let them go. I AM FREE.